Covenant Faith

Study Guide

Written by

Michael K. Lake, Th.D., D.R.E.

Chancellor, Biblical Life College and Seminary
Senior Pastor, Biblical Life Assembly
Author, The Shinar Directive: Preparing the Way for the Son of Perdition

Biblical Life Publishing

A Ministry of Biblical Life Assembly
PO Box 160 | Seymour, MO 65746-0160
Phone: 417-935-2664 | Email: biblicallife@biblical-life.net
Website: http://store.biblical-life.com

About the Author

Dr. Michael K. Lake

Chancellor and Founder, Biblical Life College & Seminary

Pastor, Biblical Life Assembly

Biblical Researcher and Best-Selling Author

A.A. - United Theological Seminary | Th.B. - Christian Bible College | Th.M. - Christian Bible Seminary | M.A. - Faith Theological Seminary | Th.D. - North American School of Theology | D.R.E. - New Covenant International Bible College

Dr. Lake is the founder of BLCS and serves as an Educational Consultant for various Christian organizations around the world. He is ordained with the Restoration Fellowship International and has served as Bishop on RFI's International Board of Directors. Dr. Lake serves as the Senior Pastor of Biblical Life Assembly in Marshfield, MO. He is listed in the U.S. Registry's "Who's Who among Outstanding Americans," Sterling's "Who's Who Executive Edition" and the "Who's Who among American Teachers" for his accomplishments in ministry and with BLCS.

Bible Translations Used:

- **KJV** – King James Bible. Public Domain.

- **TNK – JPS TANAKH** 1985 (English). The TANAKH, a new translation (into contemporary English) of The Holy Scriptures according to the traditional Hebrew text (Masoretic). The Jewish Bible: Torah, Nevi'im, Kethuvim. Copyright © 1985 by the Jewish Publication Society. All rights reserved. This fresh translation began work in 1955. Used by permission.

- **AMP** - Amplified Bible. Copyright © 1954, 1958, 1962, 1964, 1965, 1987 by The Lockman Foundation, La Habra, CA 90631

- **CJB** – Complete Jewish Bible. Copyright © 1998 by David H. Stern. Jewish New Testament Publications, Clarksville, MD 21029

Table of Contents

Module Overview

Undergraduate Level Instructions

You will need the following to successfully complete this course:

1.   This Study Guide.

2.   Covenant Faith Lectures: 16 lectures on either CD or MP3 CD.

3.   **Collateral Reading**:

Our Lost Legacy: Christianity's Hebraic Heritage by Dr. John Garr. Golden Keys Press, Atlanta, GA. ISBN: 978-0967827926. Note: Author is BLCS graduate.

4.   Final Exam.

Steps to Completing This Course

1.   Read through the notes to each lesson and then listen to the audio lecture. Take notes on significant information from the lecture that are not contained in the notes.

2.   Answer the lesson review questions at the end of the lesson. Once you have completed the questions, check them with the answers at the back of the workbook. [The workbook is self-graded. These questions are to help prepare you for the final exam.] Continue with each lesson until you have finished all 16 lessons.

3.   Read through the collateral reading book and develop a 15-page paper on significant insights you gained from the book as well as steps you plan to implement those insights.

4.   Mail in the resealed final exam and the book report together for grading.

THIS COURSE IS WORTH THREE SEMESTER CREDIT HOURS

Graduate Level Instructions

You will need the following to successfully complete this course:

1.   This Study Guide.

2.   Covenant Faith Lectures: 16 lectures on either CD or MP3 CD.

3.   **Collateral Reading**:

> Our Lost Legacy: Christianity's Hebraic Heritage by Dr. John Garr. Golden Keys Press, Atlanta, GA. ISBN: 978-0967827926. Note: Author is BLCS graduate.

Second book is student's choice. Must be at least 250 pages in length.

4.   Final Exam.

Steps to Completing This Course

1.   Read through the notes to each lesson and then listen to the audio lecture. Take notes on significant information from the lecture that are not contained in the notes.

2.   Answer the lesson review questions at the end of the lesson. Once you have completed the questions, check them with the answers at the back of the workbook. [The workbook is self-graded. These questions are to help prepare you for the final exam.] Continue with each lesson until you have finished all 16 lessons.

3.   Read through collateral reading books. Now develop a 15-page paper on significant insights you gained from each book as well as steps you plan to implement those insights.

4.   Mail in the resealed final exam and the book reports reading together for grading.

THIS COURSE IS WORTH THREE SEMESTER CREDIT HOURS

Covenant Faith – Lesson One

Introduction & Foundational Issues - Part 1

Introduction

The state of the Body of Christ today is an interesting one. Part of the Body is asleep at the wheel, just going through the motions with little hope of things getting better until they get to Heaven. Another part of the Body knows deep in their hearts that something is wrong. There should be more to their walk with God, and they realize that the traditional Church has wandered so far off the path established by God that they cannot even see the original path anymore. The latter have been awakened by the Holy Spirit to their Hebraic heritage, and it is happening in greater numbers worldwide every day.

This course is also about returning to the power of God, miracles, answered prayer, divine protection, divine provision, communion with God, and a host of other things on God's terms - not ours!

Putting Faith Back in Its Place

It is time to put faith back in its place. Faith was made to rest on the power of Covenant. Faith is not a force in itself; rather, it is an expression of covenant. If you separate faith from covenant, it becomes a force of the soul and of the flesh. In other words, it becomes a force of witchcraft and the Word of God becomes little more than sets of formulas to get what your flesh wants or a book of spells.

Faith must rest upon covenant, and covenant must rest upon a foundation made up of two things:

- Grace
- Commandments

This may sound like a contradiction to modern theology, and it is. Our modern theologies have also got us into the mess we are in today. It is time to take a thorough look at the Word of God and begin to return to the truth of God!

I.   A Foundation to Understanding God

God is complete in and of Himself as there is nothing He needs, or ever will need. He does not need creation to worship and glorify Him, nor does He need any kind of being to help Him in any way. God existed before creation and did not need humanity to boast in Him, but only allowed creation to boast in Him.[1]

God is complete in Himself. He does not need Heaven, angels, this universe, or man. He did not create anything because He needed something. All of creation is an expression of the Grace of God.

---

[1] Dewalt, Michael. The Self-Sufficiency of God. Article. http://gospelcenteredmusings.com/2009/11/11/the-self-sufficiency-of-god/

II. Creation by Grace and Commands

Genesis 1:3-5 (KJV)
[3] And God said, Let there be light: and there was light. [4] And God saw the light, that *it was* good: and God divided the light from the darkness. [5] And God called the light Day, and the darkness he called Night. And the evening and the morning were the first day.

God entered into creation because of His grace. The very essence of creation is built upon that grace and responding to the commands of God.

- God commanded that there would be light and light became!
- God commanded light to separate from darkness and it was so.

The first five days of creation were accomplished by the commands of God. At the elemental level, all of creation responds to the commands of God!

Within a command from God is the power for both its fulfillment and its maintenance.

Hebrews 1:3 (KJV)
[3] Who being the brightness of *his* glory, and the express image of his person, and upholding all things by the word of his power, when he had by himself purged our sins, sat down on the right hand of the Majesty on high;

III. Man

Genesis 2:7 (KJV)
[7] And the LORD God formed man *of* the dust of the ground, and breathed into his nostrils the breath of life; and man became a living soul.

Genesis 1:26-28 (KJV)
[26] And God said, Let us make man in our image, after our likeness: and let them have dominion over the fish of the sea, and over the fowl of the air, and over the cattle, and over all the earth, and over every creeping thing that creepeth upon the earth. [27] So God created man in his *own* image, in the image of God created he him; male and female created he them. [28] And God blessed them, and God said unto them, Be fruitful, and multiply, and replenish the earth, and subdue it: and have dominion over the fish of the sea, and over the fowl of the air, and over every living thing that moveth upon the earth.

1. Man was created by the grace of God. God did not need anything that man could give Him.

2. Man came into existence by the breath of God. Man longs to be continually filled with the Spirit (breath) of God.

Living: Strongs # H**2416** חַי chay {khah'-ee} [2]
Meaning: adj 1) <u>living, alive</u> 1a) green (of vegetation) 1b) flowing, fresh (of water) 1c) lively, active (of man) 1d) reviving (of the springtime) n m 2) relatives 3) life (abstract emphatic) 3a) life 3b) <u>sustenance, maintenance</u> n f 4) living thing, animal 4a) animal 4b) life 4c) appetite 4d) <u>revival, renewal</u> 5) community
Origin: from 02421; TWOT - 644a

Man's sustenance and maintenance to real life are found in prayer and in true worship. Through prayer and worship we have access to the Spirit of God.

3.　　　The first thing given to man was commandments:

- Be fruitful and multiply
- Replenish the Earth.
- Subdue It.
- Take dominion over creation

God later added to those commandments:

Genesis 2:15-17 (KJV)
[15] And the LORD God took the man, and put him into the garden of Eden to dress it and to keep it. [16] And the LORD God commanded the man, saying, Of every tree of the garden thou mayest freely eat: [17] But of the tree of the knowledge of good and evil, thou shalt not eat of it: for in the day that thou eatest thereof thou shalt surely die.

- Cultivate the Garden.
- Watch over the Garden and guard it.
- Do not eat of this one tree.

> It is within the spiritual DNA of man to be filled with the Spirit of God and to function within the commandments of God – all by the grace of God. If you separate man from God's grace, God's Spirit, or God's commandments, he cannot function properly!

Review

All of creation, to include man, was an expression of God's Grace.

All of creation is designed to respond to the commandments of God.

For man to really be alive, he requires three things:
- God's Grace
- God's Spirit
- God's Commandments

---

[2] Strong's Enhanced Lexicon. BibleWorks for Windows 7.0. BibleWorks, LLC, Norfolk, VA. Copyright © 2006.

If we deny any of these, we have reduced our function in both the earth and in God's Kingdom, and we have fallen short of the life God intended for us!

Review Questions

1. How is grace connected to creation and His commandments?

2. Was man given commandments in the Garden before the fall? If so, what were they?

3. What is encoded into the spiritual DNA of man?

Covenant Faith - Lesson Two

I.   The Mosaic of God's Word Distorted

God has revealed Himself, His ways, His Kingdom, and our need for Him through His Word. It is a beautiful Mosaic of stories and teachings that reveal to us concepts and principles to live successfully now and in Eternity. God must slowly reveal them to us from beginning to end:

Isaiah 28:9-10 (KJV)
[9] Whom shall he teach knowledge? and whom shall he make to understand doctrine? *them that are* weaned from the milk, *and* drawn from the breasts. [10] For precept *must be* upon precept, precept upon precept; line upon line, line upon line; here a little, *and* there a little:

If we fail to connect the dots and understand the layers, God goes on to tell us:

Isaiah 28:12-13 (KJV)
[12] To whom he said, This *is* the rest *wherewith* ye may cause the weary to rest; and this *is* the refreshing: <u>yet they would not hear</u>. [13] But the word of the LORD was unto them precept upon precept, precept upon precept; line upon line, line upon line; here a little, *and* there a little; that they might go, and fall backward, and be broken, and snared, and taken.

How is it that we would not hear?

We throw out concepts and principles that we do not like. We take certain concepts that we like and stretch them with such emphasis that they are distorted well beyond the bounds of God's Word, and they no longer resemble what God was trying to say.

> We turn God's mosaic into an abstract that Heaven can no longer recognize, but Hell delights in!

II.   Patterns and Covenants

We found out in our last lesson that from the very beginning God always starts with grace. Following grace are commandments to be walked in BECAUSE of the grace bestowed upon us. Adam had commandments in the Garden before the fall that were designed to bless him, empower him, and to protect him.

Covenants

As I began to study covenants for this series, I was amused at what previous authors called covenant. Most theologians say that there was the Edenic Covenant in Genesis before the fall. They ignore the fact that both Torah and Hebrews 9 teach us that covenant requires a sacrifice. This is one of the reasons that the main covenants in the Word of God are blood covenants: they were established by the shedding of blood.

In the Garden, Adam did not have a covenant with God; rather, he had a commission. Covenant usually means that you are in a weakened state and need the grace of someone stronger to come into covenant with. God did not create Adam in a weakened state. Adam was empowered by God and given the authority to take dominion over this planet!

It was only when man fell that God had to initiate covenant. Covenant is always extended from the Almighty because of His grace either toward mankind or an individual.

III. The Fall of Mankind

Genesis 3:8-24 (KJV)
[8] And they heard the voice of the LORD God walking in the garden in the cool of the day: and Adam and his wife hid themselves from the presence of the LORD God amongst the trees of the garden. [9] And the LORD God called unto Adam, and said unto him, Where *art* thou? [10] And he said, I heard thy voice in the garden, and I was afraid, because I *was* naked; and I hid myself. [11] And he said, Who told thee that thou *wast* naked? Hast thou eaten of the tree, whereof I commanded thee that thou shouldest not eat? [12] And the man said, The woman whom thou gavest *to be* with me, she gave me of the tree, and I did eat. [13] And the LORD God said unto the woman, What *is* this *that* thou hast done? And the woman said, The serpent beguiled me, and I did eat. [14] And the LORD God said unto the serpent, Because thou hast done this, thou *art* cursed above all cattle, and above every beast of the field; upon thy belly shalt thou go, and dust shalt thou eat all the days of thy life: [15] And I will put enmity between thee and the woman, and between thy seed and her seed; it shall bruise thy head, and thou shalt bruise his heel. [16] Unto the woman he said, I will greatly multiply thy sorrow and thy conception; in sorrow thou shalt bring forth children; and thy desire *shall be* to thy husband, and he shall rule over thee. [17] And unto Adam he said, Because thou hast hearkened unto the voice of thy wife, and hast eaten of the tree, of which I commanded thee, saying, Thou shalt not eat of it: cursed *is* the ground for thy sake; in sorrow shalt thou eat *of* it all the days of thy life; [18] Thorns also and thistles shall it bring forth to thee; and thou shalt eat the herb of the field; [19] In the sweat of thy face shalt thou eat bread, till thou return unto the ground; for out of it wast thou taken: for dust thou *art*, and unto dust shalt thou return. [20] And Adam called his wife's name Eve; because she was the mother of all living. [21] Unto Adam also and to his wife did the LORD God make coats of skins, and clothed them. [22] And the LORD God said, Behold, the man is become as one of us, to know good and evil: and now, lest he put forth his hand, and take also of the tree of life, and eat, and live for ever: [23] Therefore the LORD God sent him forth from the garden of Eden, to till the ground from whence he was taken. [24] So he drove out the man; and he placed at the east of the garden of Eden Cherubims, and a flaming sword which turned every way, to keep the way of the tree of life.

a. **Adam Where Art Thou?:** Dr. Karl Coke, our Hebrew professor at Biblical Life, tells us that this is not an accurate translation of the Hebrew. It should read, "So Adam, how's it working out for you?" Man chose his own path and violated the commandments of God. In doing so, he committed high treason against the Most High.

b. **The Blame Game**: It is almost instinctual for man, when he does something he knows he should not have done, to play the blame game. Adam had all that authority, used it to go against God, and yet would not take responsibility for it!

c. **God Setting Things Right for the Woman**: In 1 Timothy 2:14, God tells us that Adam was not deceived. He knew exactly what he was doing. On the other hand, Eve was deceived and thought she was doing something good. The Messianic Promise was given to Eve, not Adam. Since Eve was created to submit and have relationship (which before the serpent included only God and Adam), God refined who she was supposed to submit to: her own husband. This was not a curse; it was a commandment to protect her!

d. **Man's Work Now Has Resistance**: Because of man's rebellion and sin, resistance would come against his work in the earth. As we will see, the only way for man to overcome this resistance would be (1) the grace of God, and (2) the commandments of God.

e. **Blood Covenant Alluded To**: When God provided the skins of animals for Adam and Eve to wear, all theologians believe this was God showing man that sacrifice must be accomplished because of his sin. This is for two reasons: (1) God would not waste the innocent life of the animals just for clothing: there had to be more to it, and (2) Cain and Able both already understood what a proper sacrifice was in Genesis 4.

The Adamic Covenant was a blood covenant that promised one day God would fix the mess that man had gotten himself into by violating the commandments of God.

IV.   A Fresh Look at Commandments

In the Twenty-First century, we were embedded with the errors of Marcion, and later by Catholic theology, to believe that the commandments of God were bad and not for us. Let's take another look at the commandments in the Garden.

In the Garden, the commandments of God:

- Gave man authority and dominion.
- Created the framework for man to conduct his commission in the earth.
- Gave man the grounds to legally protect himself and his wife in the Garden.
- Created an atmosphere for God to come and fellowship with him.

When man violated the commandments of God:

- He gave away his authority and dominion to Satan, and Satan became the god of this world.
- He destroyed the framework for man to conduct his commission in the earth.
- Man lost the legal grounds to protect himself and his wife spiritually and physically.
- Man destroyed the fellowship and communion he had with God.

No wonder Hell hates the commandments of God so much!

What About Not Being Saved by Works?

Ephesians 2:8-10 (KJV)
[8] For by grace are ye saved through faith; and that not of yourselves: *it is* the gift of God: [9] <u>Not of works</u>, lest any man should boast. [10] For we are his workmanship, <u>created in Christ Jesus unto good works, which God hath before ordained that we should walk in them</u>.

Several issues to deal with here:

Was man created by the grace of God or by keeping commandments? Grace came first. Same in salvation: grace, then commandments.

What works was Paul dealing with? Was man trying to "earn" his salvation? No. Paul was specifically dealing with the error of some of the Pharisees in Acts 15:1:

> **Acts 15:1 (KJV)**
> [1] And certain men which came down from Judaea taught the brethren, *and said*, Except ye be circumcised after the manner of Moses, ye cannot be saved.

God's pattern is: Grace THEN commandments!

If Paul was not dealing with people trying to earn their salvation in New Testament times, then where did we get this concept? - The Catholic Church and the concept of "penitence." Protestants over the centuries have transferred this concept from being of Catholic origin to Jewish. No Hebrew from Abraham on ever thought they could earn God's forgiveness! **We are reading concepts into scripture that were never there!**

Paul tells us that we are not saved by works (keeping commandments), but in the salvation process we are recreated in Messiah to keep the commandments.

> **Ephesians 2:8-10 (AMP)**
> [8] For it is by free grace (God's unmerited favor) that you are saved (delivered from judgment *and* made partakers of Christ's salvation) through [your] faith. And this [salvation] is not of yourselves [of your own doing, it came not through your own striving], but it is the gift of God; [9] Not because of works [not the fulfillment of the Law's demands], lest any man should boast. [It is not the result of what anyone can possibly do, so no one can pride himself in it or take glory to himself.] [10] For we are God's [own] handiwork (His workmanship), recreated in Christ Jesus, [born anew] that we may do those good works which God predestined (planned beforehand) for us [taking paths which He prepared ahead of time], that we should walk in them [living the good life which He prearranged and made ready for us to live].

Review Questions

1.   How has man made God's Word an abstract rather than a Mosaic?

2.   Was there an Edenic covenant?

3.   How are keeping commandments not being saved by works?

Covenant Faith – Lesson Three

Introduction

God is always faithful to give you the right piece of the puzzle at the precise moment you need it. It can come from a book, a clip from a sermon, or even a thesis one is grading. This week, God dropped another piece of the puzzle of powerful covenant faith into my lap through a thesis from a BLCS student named Chad. Chad's thesis is entitled "Restoring Foundations: Rediscovering the Truths of Covenants and Torah." (We are helping him publish this thesis, and it will become required reading for this course!). Here is what Chad shared that so stood out to me:

> "According to Scripture, believing God means that we hear the word He speaks and change our lives to match His Word, and live our lives trusting that His word is sure, truthful, and life-giving. We see this type of belief in the life of Abraham.
>
> Believing God will change your life. If you think you have believed God about a Scriptural truth and it does not change your life, you probably have only mental assent to a spiritual law. Giving mental assent to a law could be compared to someone coming up to a red stoplight, acknowledging they should stop, and then driving through it. Those who really believe a stoplight is important will stop if it is red, even at 2 AM when no one else is around. If we truly believe God, we will listen closely to what He says, we will trust Him, and we will obey Him: even when no one else is around.
>
> I don't know if this can be overemphasized. Believing God is critical. If you do not believe God, you will not be able to make a covenant with Him, Jesus will not be your Lord and Savior, and if you die in unbelief, you will spend eternity in hell. Believe God!"[3]

I. Adding to the Pattern

To get to covenant, you must be visited by the Grace of God, hearing His voice (i.e. given commandment), obey the commandment from your heart, and then begin establishing this covenant in

---

[3] Kottke, Chad. Restoring Foundations: Rediscovering Truths of Covenant and Torah. Thesis submitted to Biblical Life College and Seminary toward the Master of Divinity degree. Copyright 2011. Page 8.

your life. The deeper and stronger the covenant becomes, the more you will hear God's voice, the more instruction (or commandments) you will receive, the more you will lovingly obey His instruction, and the more you will reap the blessings of covenant!

Changing our paradigm about God's commandments:

a.   Greek meaning of law is oppressive and bad.

b.   Law or Torah in Hebrew is completely different!

> **Torah:** Strongs # **8451** תּוֹרָה towrah {to-raw'} or תֹּרָה torah {to-raw'}[4]
> **Meaning:** 1) law, direction, instruction 1a) instruction, direction (human or divine) 1a1) body of prophetic teaching 1a2) instruction in Messianic age 1a3) body of priestly direction or instruction 1a4) body of legal directives 1b) law 1b1) law of the burnt offering 1b2) of special law, codes of law 1c) custom, manner 1d) the Deuteronomic or Mosaic Law.

Theological Workbook of the Old Testament – Moody Press

> **Scope of the Word . . .**
>
> The word *târâ* means basically "teaching" whether it is the wise man instructing his son or God instructing Israel. The wise give insight into all aspects of life so that the young may know how to conduct themselves and to live a long blessed life (Proverbs 3:1f.). So too God, motivated by love, reveals to man basic insight into how to live with each other and how to approach God. Through the law God shows his interest in all aspects of man's life which is to be lived under his direction and care. Law of God stands parallel to word of the Lord to signify that law is the revelation of God's will (e.g. Isaiah 1:10). In this capacity it becomes the nation's wisdom and understanding so that others will marvel at the quality of Israel's distinctive lifestyle (Deut. 4:6). Thus, there is a very similar understanding of the role of teaching with its results in the wisdom school, in the priestly instruction, and the role of the law with its results for all the people of the covenant. [5]

II.   Looking Back at the Fall Again

Genesis 3:1-5 (KJV)
[1] Now the serpent was more subtil than any beast of the field which the LORD God had made. And he said unto the woman, Yea, hath God said, Ye shall not eat of every tree of the garden? [2] And the woman said unto the serpent, We may eat of the fruit of the trees of the garden: [3] But of the fruit of the tree which *is* in the midst of the garden, God hath said, Ye shall not eat of it, neither shall ye touch it, lest ye die. [4] And the serpent said unto the woman, Ye shall not surely die: [5] For God doth know that in the day ye eat thereof, then your eyes shall be opened, and ye shall be as gods, knowing good and evil.

- Satan questioned God's instruction and God's motives. (Just like today!)

---

[4] Strong's Enhanced Lexicon. BibleWorks for Windows 7.0. BibleWorks, LLC, Norfolk, VA. Copyright © 2006.
[5] R. Laird Harris, Gleason L. Archer, Bruce K. Waltke, ed., "910: יָרָה," in *Theological Wordbook of the Old Testament*, (Chicago: Moody Press, 1980), WORDsearch CROSS e-book, 404.

- Satan established the lie that God's instruction was designed to hold us back rather than to keep us safe.
- Satan provided a different instruction (or command).

We need to understand that when God gave man free-will, that man became the doorkeeper to his own life. Whatever he listens to and obeys, he opens the door to in his life. Whatever he chooses to disobey, he closes the door to.

Matthew 16:19 (KJV)
[19] And I will give unto thee the keys of the kingdom of heaven: and whatsoever thou shalt bind on earth shall be bound in heaven: and whatsoever thou shalt loose on earth shall be loosed in heaven.

In the Garden, man fell and lost his free will. Man could no longer choose to obey God unless he was touched by God's grace. Jesus was telling His disciples that, through His completed work, He was restoring their power to choose! He was again reminding them that they were the door-keepers to their own lives once again!

II.   Seeing the Pattern with Noah

Genesis 6:8-9 (KJV)
[8] But Noah found grace in the eyes of the LORD. [9] These *are* the generations of Noah: Noah was a just man *and* perfect in his generations, *and* Noah walked with God.

God extended His grace to Noah and walked with him. In this grace, God gave commandments to Noah to prepare for the judgment of God. Noah heard the voice of God, obeyed it, and his faith built an ark of safety that would ride out the storm of God's judgment on a world filled with sin and corruption!

Genesis 8:20-22 (KJV)
[20] And Noah builded an altar unto the LORD; and took of every clean beast, and of every clean fowl, and offered burnt offerings on the altar. [21] And the LORD smelled a sweet savour; and the LORD said in his heart, I will not again curse the ground any more for man's sake; for the imagination of man's heart *is* evil from his youth; neither will I again smite any more every thing living, as I have done. [22] While the earth remaineth, seedtime and harvest, and cold and heat, and summer and winter, and day and night shall not cease.

Genesis 9:8-11 (KJV)
[8] And God spake unto Noah, and to his sons with him, saying, [9] And I, behold, I establish my covenant with you, and with your seed after you; [10] And with every living creature that *is* with you, of the fowl, of the cattle, and of every beast of the earth with you; from all that go out of the ark, to every beast of the earth. [11] And I will establish my covenant with you; neither shall all flesh be cut off any more by the waters of a flood; neither shall there any more be a flood to destroy the earth.

Review Questions

1.   Hearing commandment + _____ = Faith

2.   What is the biblical concept of "Law"?

3.   Does the pattern "of hearing plus doing equals faith" line up with the story of Noah? If so, how?

Covenant Faith – Lesson Four

The Transformation of Abram – Part 1

Introduction

I believe that the greatest human potential in the world exists within the Body of Christ. Unfortunately, as one views Christian history over the past one hundred years, the Christians that have gone from ordinary to extraordinary have become fewer with each generation. **I believe that the kingdom of darkness has found a way to impede believers from reaching their potential in Christ**!

We are living in a time where the philosophy of many is: "the end justifies the means." From trade unions to churches to governments, we can see this mentality. This flawed concept is being pushed in our schools, unions, community organizations, and government based upon a book called "Rules for Radicals" by Saul Alinsky. In his book dedication, he writes:

> "Lest we forget at least an over-the-shoulder acknowledgement to the very first radical: from all our legends, mythology, and history (and who is to know where mythology leaves off and history begins – or which is which), the first radical known to man who rebelled against the establishment and did so effectively that he at least won his own kingdom – Lucifer."

Alinsky actually gives us a hint to where he drew his knowledge from. The "end justifies the means" concept is found in two of the three temptations of Jesus in the wilderness. Jesus rejected this concept because it never ends well. The truth is:

> "Who you become during the journey is as important (if not more) as where you are headed."

> *It is in the journey that you become who you are going to be and the fullness of your potential is released.*

Hebrews 12:1-2 (KJV)
[1] Wherefore seeing we also are compassed about with so great a cloud of witnesses, let us lay aside every weight, and the sin which doth so easily beset *us*, and let us run with patience the race that is set before us, [2] Looking unto Jesus the author and finisher of *our* faith; who for the joy that was set before him endured the cross, despising the shame, and is set down at the right hand of the throne of God.

We have seen too many believers that have their eyes on Heaven but have been sold the lie that there is no journey to be walked out here. We have forgotten what previous generations knew so well: *in the journey is transformation*!

I believe this is why the Apostle Paul chose the example of Abraham so many times in his writings to the Gentiles. Abram started out a Gentile, but in the journey, he became the man that was a friend of God!

I. You've Got to Get Out of Here!

Genesis 12:1 (KJV)
[1] Now the LORD had said unto Abram, Get thee out of thy country, and from thy kindred, and from thy father's house, unto a land that I will shew thee:

Abram was a citizen of Babylon. His father, according to the rabbis, was a maker of idols. In other words, Abram was a pagan in every sense of the word. When God entered into his life, it was because of grace. As soon as God reached out to Abram in His grace, He gave a command to leave Babylon behind forever!

Principle # 1 in biblical transformation is to leave Babylon behind!

You cannot hold on to Babylon and expect transformation! Satan has done such an exceptional job of embedding Babylon into the Church. Through our extra-biblical holidays that originated in Babylon to worldly philosophies that we have embraced, he has brought biblical transformation to a screeching halt in the Church. Believers are still in the chains of Babylon's influence and dreaming of Heaven. But in the transformation, we can have some of Heaven now!

Deuteronomy 11:18-21 (KJV)
[18] Therefore shall ye lay up these my words in your heart and in your soul, and bind them for a sign upon your hand, that they may be as frontlets between your eyes. [19] And ye shall teach them your children, speaking of them when thou sittest in thine house, and when thou walkest by the way, when thou liest down, and when thou risest up. [20] And thou shalt write them upon the door posts of thine house, and upon thy gates: [21] That your days may be multiplied, and the days of your children, in the land which the LORD sware unto your fathers to give them, <u>as the days of heaven upon the earth.</u>

John 10:9-10 (KJV)
[9] I am the door: by me if any man enter in, he shall be saved, and shall go in and out, and find pasture. [10] The thief cometh not, but for to steal, and to kill, and to destroy: I am come that they might have life, and that they might have *it* more abundantly.

Our Trends Are In All the Wrong Directions

We have given up on the dream of transformation and have replaced it with materialism. The Laodicean Church is alive and well in Western civilization! We fight to keep Babylonian traditions that appease our flesh and fight not to embrace the instruction of God (Torah) that requires its crucifixion! Now the very ones that can be transformed by the Hand of God are fighting the transformation and have been sold the lie that status quo is all that one can hope for!

Colossians 1:12-14 (KJV)
[12] Giving thanks unto the Father, which hath made us meet to be partakers of the inheritance of the saints in light: [13] Who hath delivered us from the power of darkness, and hath translated *us* into the kingdom of his dear Son: [14] In whom we have redemption through his blood, *even* the forgiveness of sins:

II.   I Will Make Thee

Genesis 12:2 (KJV)
[2] And <u>I will make of thee</u> a great nation, and I will bless thee, and make thy name great; and thou shalt be a blessing:

There is so much that we have missed in this verse. The end result was that God was going to make a great nation from Abram, <u>but God first had to make Abram a man that could father a great nation</u>! The journey that Abram took was a journey into transformation to become that man!

Blessed to Bless

Today believers are seeking after the blessing of God as if the blessing was the end goal. With that attitude, they use the blessings of God to feed their flesh, and they become the Church in Laodicea! ***Materialism can mimic spirituality***.

Abram quickly realized that what God was doing in his life was more than just about himself. The transformation and the blessing were for future generations. That is faith! That is the call of Abram. That is what we all share in both Abram and Jesus! Who we become in Christ has more effect on the world around us than anything else. No wonder Satan has fought so hard against biblical transformation!

III.   The Place of Transformation and Spiritual Warfare

Genesis 12:3 (KJV)
[3] And I will bless them that bless thee, and curse him that curseth thee: and in thee shall all families of the earth be blessed.

Those that are touched by the grace of God and have left Babylon behind find themselves in the best place to conduct spiritual warfare for the Kingdom. God will begin fighting on their behalf. It takes a while to get there and a while to learn how to walk in it. This is something that Abram had to learn.

In warfare, a soldier can call in cover fire or even air support. Yes, we will have to fight some battles, but God will give us air support that throws the enemy off balance so we can survive and press on to transformation and victory!

Review Questions

1.   What is the purpose of the journey?

2.   How has Satan brought spiritual transformation to a halt?

3.   How can materialism mimic spirituality?

Covenant Faith – Lesson Five

The Transformation of Abram – Part 2

I.   Beginning to Build Faith

Genesis 12:7 (KJV)
[7] And the LORD appeared unto Abram, and said, Unto thy seed will I give this land: and there builded he an altar unto the LORD, who appeared unto him.

Once Abram was touched by the grace of God and began to move in obedience to the voice (commands of God), God visited him again. This time God began to work on building the faith of Abram. God did two things:

- He promised Abram a descendant (Remember Gen. 11:30 told us that Sarai was barren).

- He promised Abram that his descendant would receive all this land from His hand.

__Mountain moving faith always begins where man's abilities end!__

We need to realize that faith is always about obtaining the impossible. If it is within our reach, it is not faith: it is our abilities.

__God had to stretch Abram beyond where he was to make room for where God wanted him to be__:

Before God can move us on, He must make us bigger on the inside. Heart, vision, compassion, endurance, faith, etc. that move mountains and overcome every adversity are elements built within man. Without these internal spiritual characteristics, the world around you can never be changed!

Remember, the Kingdom of God is always built within first!

Luke 17:20-21 (KJV)
[20] And when he was demanded of the Pharisees, when the kingdom of God should come, he answered them and said, The kingdom of God cometh not with observation: [21] Neither shall they say, Lo here! or, lo there! for, behold, the kingdom of God is within you.

II.   Faith is Always Challenged

In verses 8 and 9 of Genesis 12, Abram starts moving through the land that God had promised him and builds places of worship (altars) unto God.

Then we come to verse 10:

Genesis 12:10 (KJV)
[10] And there was a famine in the land: and Abram went down into Egypt to sojourn there; for the famine *was* grievous in the land.

There is a famine in the land of promise. Have you ever felt like the promises God has given you have all dried up? This is the first challenge to the faith that God was endeavoring to build in the heart of Abram. Satan was using famine to drive him out of the very land that God had promised him.

We need to remember that Satan will challenge all promises of God and your faith. This is another pattern we see continually in the Word of God. You cannot escape it; rather, you must learn how to overcome it!

Jesus, the Word, and the Sower:

Mark 4:1-9 (KJV)
[1] And he began again to teach by the sea side: and there was gathered unto him a great multitude, so that he entered into a ship, and sat in the sea; and the whole multitude was by the sea on the land. [2] And he taught them many things by parables, and said unto them in his doctrine, [3] Hearken; Behold, there went out a sower to sow: [4] And it came to pass, as he sowed, some fell by the way side, and the fowls of the air came and devoured it up. [5] And some fell on stony ground, where it had not much earth; and immediately it sprang up, because it had no depth of earth: [6] But when the sun was up, it was scorched; and because it had no root, it withered away. [7] And some fell among thorns, and the thorns grew up, and choked it, and it yielded no fruit. [8] And other fell on good ground, and did yield fruit that sprang up and increased; and brought forth, some thirty, and some sixty, and some an hundred. [9] And he said unto them, He that hath ears to hear, let him hear.

In Mark 4, Jesus was teaching them the spiritual pattern of growth and transformation that Abram, and all those the proceeded him, must go through. Without understanding the pattern and principles, revealed both in the life of Abram and this parable, you will be frustrated and offended at God.

Mark 4:10-20 (KJV)
[10] And when he was alone, they that were about him with the twelve asked of him the parable. [11] And he said unto them, Unto you it is given to know the mystery of the kingdom of God: but unto them that are without, all *these* things are done in parables: [12] That seeing they may see, and not perceive; and hearing they may hear, and not understand; lest at any time they should be converted, and *their* sins should be forgiven them. [13] And he said unto them, Know ye not this parable? and how then will ye know all parables? [14] The sower soweth the word. [15] And these are they by the way side, where the word is sown; but when they have heard, Satan cometh immediately, and taketh away the word that was sown in their hearts. [16] And these are they likewise which are sown on stony ground; who, when they have heard the word, immediately receive it with gladness; [17] And have no root in themselves, and so endure but for a time: afterward, when affliction or persecution ariseth for the word's sake, immediately they are offended. [18] And these are they which are sown among thorns; such as hear the word, [19] And the cares of this world, and the deceitfulness of riches, and the lusts of other things entering in, choke the word, and it becometh unfruitful. [20] And these are they which are sown on good ground; such as hear the word, and receive *it*, and bring forth fruit, some thirtyfold, some sixty, and some an hundred.

It is given unto His disciples to understand the mysteries of the Kingdom:

> You need to get this down in your spirit: God is not withholding the mysteries of the Kingdom from you! I believe that many times we misunderstand how the mysteries are revealed. Mysteries are only revealed through discovery. You cannot just explain them to someone. These mysteries are discovered through both the promises of God and the trials of life. It is through the synergetic working of the two that spiritual discoveries are made!
>
> So God is not holding back; He works to move you forward to discover and revelation.

This parable is the key to understanding all of the parables of Jesus:

> If you get what Jesus is teaching here in this parable, it will unlock all of His teachings that are parable based. It is the spiritual Rosetta Stone to the understanding of the Kingdom!

Satan comes immediately to take the Word (promise):

> Get this into your spirit and mind: anytime God reveals something to you and does something in your life, Satan will come to steal it before it really takes root!

You have to work to get the promise deep into your heart and spirit!

Stony ground is an unprepared heart:

> If you showed me a garden plot that you were going to plant in and it was full of stones, I would tell you that you needed to remove the stones and till the soil to prepare it properly. It is not a matter of being glad that there is seed. Everyone loves insight and revelation, but few have prepared themselves to receive it!
>
> Just as God had to expand the inside of Abram so that He could bless him on the outside, we must also prepare room for God's promises and give them a place to take root!

Persecution and affliction arise for the Word's sake:

> ### Affliction: Strongs # G2347 θλῖψις thlipsis {thlip'-sis} [6]
> **Meaning:** 1) a pressing, pressing together, pressure 2) metaph. oppression, affliction, tribulation, distress, straits
> **Origin:** from 2346; TDNT - 3:139,334; n f
> **Usage:** AV - tribulation 21, affliction 17, trouble 3, anguish 1, persecution 1, burdened 1, to be afflicted + 1519 1; 45
>
> ### Persecution: Strongs # G1375 διωγμός diogmos {dee-ogue-mos'} [7]
> **Meaning:** 1) persecution
> **Origin:** from 1377;; n m

---

[6] Strong's Enhanced Lexicon. BibleWorks for Windows 7.0. BibleWorks, LLC, Norfolk, VA. Copyright © 2006.
[7] Strong's Enhanced Lexicon. BibleWorks for Windows 7.0. BibleWorks, LLC, Norfolk, VA. Copyright © 2006.

Usage: AV - persecution 10; 10

Satan will always put pressure on you to keep you from receiving the promises God is trying to establish in you. You must learn to push through the pressure until the promise is established.

The enemy also loves to use persecution. I have been really amazed over the years that the persecution usually comes from carnally minded believers and relatives more than the world. I have had sinners say "If that's what you believe, go for it!" While saints that have taken up permanent residency in God's nursery begin telling you how crazy you are for believing the Word and then start the gossip mill against you.

It all comes down to who is going to fulfill the promise? Is it the naysayers around you or God?

Cares of this world, deceitfulness of riches, and the lusts of other things:

Cares: Strongs #G3308 μέριμνα merimna {mer'-im-nah}[8]
Meaning: 1) care, anxiety
Origin: from 3307 (through the idea of distraction); TDNT - 4:589,584; n f
Usage: AV - care 6; 6

The New American Standard Bible translates this as "worries." We need to realize that as long as we are in this world, there will ALWAYS be something to worry about. The things that cause the worries are why we need God, His promises, His power, and faith! We can either concentrate on the problems or the promises to overcome them. We add power to what we concentrate on!

Deception of Wealth:

I have been concerned about just how much emphasis is placed within sections of the Body of Christ on wealth and how that wealth proves one's spirituality. Overemphasis and trust in wealth always opens the door to deception. As the Laodicean Church found out in Revelation, the deception that can come with wealth will choke out true spirituality and spiritual growth. Use wealth when God blesses you with it. Never trust in it or chase after it. If we are going to chase after anything, let it be God!

Lust of Other Things:

Lust: Strongs # G1939 ἐπιθυμία epithumia {ep-ee-thoo-mee'-ah} [9]
Meaning: 1) desire, craving, longing, desire for what is forbidden, lust
Origin: from 1937; TDNT - 3:168,339; n f
Usage: AV - lust 31, concupiscence 3, desire 3, lust after 1; 38
Misc: For Synonyms see entry 5845

Lust or desire comes in several varieties. There can be an overemphasis on good things that can choke out the place for God's promises. (Remember, you only have room for

---

[8] Strong's Enhanced Lexicon. BibleWorks for Windows 7.0. BibleWorks, LLC, Norfolk, VA. Copyright © 2006.
[9] Strong's Enhanced Lexicon. BibleWorks for Windows 7.0. BibleWorks, LLC, Norfolk, VA. Copyright © 2006.

so much in your inner and outer world!). Then desires can be revealed as things that are forbidden by God. These things not only choke out what God is trying to establish in your life, but can destroy any progress you have already made!

Pay the price to be good ground:

When God begins to build something in your life, fight to establish it! Clear away the stones and the thorns. Expect persecution and pressure and make provision to overcome it! Guard against cares, worries, deception, and desires for other things! What God wants to do is so much more important than all of these! Only then can you begin producing and growing in the Kingdom!

Review Questions

1. Where does mountain moving-faith begin?

2. Is it normal to have your faith and the promises of God challenged?

3. How do we protect ourselves from these challenges?

Covenant Faith – Lesson Six

The Transformation of Abram – Part 3

Quick Review

1.   God came to Abram because of grace. Whenever God comes on the scene, He always brings grace with Him. The only exception is for those that consistently reject His grace; He will eventually show up with judgment.

2.   After you are touched by God's grace, He gives instruction. The grace was given to empower you to respond and obey the instruction He gives.

3.   Obedience to God's instruction releases promises into your life! God's grace and love are unconditional, but His promises are always conditional. Every command or instruction of God has a promise encapsulated in it. There is no way to get to the promise without obedience!

4.   Satan fears the results that the promise can bring, so he will always come and use various methods to move you away from obedience and THE PROMISE. A promise established is (1) impossible to remove, and (2) will move from generation to generation. The promises God wants to establish in you are always more than just about you! Remember: Blessed and to be a blessing!

I.   What's Going On with Abram?

Genesis 12:10-13 (KJV)
[10] And there was a famine in the land: and Abram went down into Egypt to sojourn there; for the famine *was* grievous in the land. [11] And it came to pass, when he was come near to enter into Egypt, that he said unto Sarai his wife, Behold now, I know that thou *art* a fair woman to look upon: [12] Therefore it shall come to pass, when the Egyptians shall see thee, that they shall say, This *is* his wife: and they will kill me, but they will save thee alive. [13] Say, I pray thee, thou *art* my sister: that it may be well with me for thy sake; and my soul shall live because of thee.

The Word of God is written in such a way that it is supposed to generate questions. When we do not ask the questions, the Word cannot take us to the conclusions we need through its reading!

What's going on with Abram?

- Was Sarai that fine that the Pharaoh would have killed him for her? (Was she a Middle Eastern super model?)

- Was this the reputation of the Pharaoh, and did he love to collect beautiful women?

- Was this an inner fear of Abram that someone rich and powerful would draw Sarai away from him?

- Was this a self-fulfilling prophecy?

- Did Satan use the fears of Abram to speak this situation into existence?

One thing is certain: Abram was still thinking like someone from Babylon and was still growing in the fact of who he now was in God!

II.   God's Got Your Back, Even When You Miss It!

Genesis 12:14-20 (KJV)
[14] And it came to pass, that, when Abram was come into Egypt, the Egyptians beheld the woman that she *was* very fair. [15] The princes also of Pharaoh saw her, and commended her before Pharaoh: and the woman was taken into Pharaoh's house. [16] And he entreated Abram well for her sake: and he had sheep, and oxen, and he asses, and menservants, and maidservants, and she asses, and camels. [17] And the LORD plagued Pharaoh and his house with great plagues because of Sarai Abram's wife. [18] And Pharaoh called Abram, and said, What *is* this *that* thou hast done unto me? why didst thou not tell me that she *was* thy wife? [19] Why saidst thou, She *is* my sister? so I might have taken her to me to wife: now therefore behold thy wife, take *her*, and go thy way. [20] And Pharaoh commanded *his* men concerning him: and they sent him away, and his wife, and all that he had.

Abram's prophetic evaluation of the circumstances in Egypt was playing out just like he expected, except God had his back!

We need to realize that when we faithfully respond to God's grace through obedience and the promise is released, God allows us a learning curve to grow into the person that can walk in the promise!

You never start out being the person that can walk into the promises God wants to release into your life. If you were, you would not have needed the grace God initially gave you! The grace was there because:

- You did not deserve it.
- You could not produce it.
- You could not walk in it.
- You could not maintain it!

Grace and God's commandments do several things:

- They open the doors to God's impossible.
- They begin transforming you to walk in God's impossible.
- They protect you as you become one that can live in God's impossible!

Faithfulness to what God is establishing in you is the key!

God Intervened!

According to Egyptian belief, Pharaoh was a god in the land: the authority and person of Osiris was resident within his body. <u>Yet the height of Egyptian (and masonic) working was plagued by God to protect one moving toward promise</u>!

 Important Note: When you are faithful to the grace and instruction of God and God is moving you toward the promise, He will treat you like you are already there!

Powerful Statement about Abram

Genesis 13:1-4 (KJV)
[1] And Abram went up out of Egypt, he, and his wife, and all that he had, and Lot with him, into the south. [2] And Abram *was* very rich in cattle, in silver, and in gold. [3] And he went on his journeys from the south even to Bethel, unto the place where his tent had been at the beginning, between Bethel and Hai; [4] Unto the place of the altar, which he had made there at the first: and there Abram called on the name of the LORD.

1.   The wealth of Egypt went with him as he moved back toward his promise.

       This is a very powerful prophetic picture that will be reproduced again and again for those that follow the faith of Abram. When his children left Egypt (they entered because of famine), they also left with the riches of the land!

2.   Abram knew that he messed up and returned back to the place where he first heard God.

       We will all stumble in our walk toward the promise. Do not let pride keep you from returning to the place you first heard God, and then move forward again from there.

       God will not speak to you at your place of disobedience. He will only speak in your place of obedience. You will have to return (repent) to hear again!

       Revelation 2:5 (KJV)
       [5] Remember therefore from whence thou art fallen, and **<u>repent</u>**, and **<u>do the first works</u>**; or else I will come unto thee quickly, and will remove thy candlestick out of his place, except thou repent.

Review Questions

1.   Can our self-doubts become self-fulfilling prophecies?

2.   How does God's grace have our backs when our self-doubt causes us to mess up?

3.   Why is it so important to return to the place of obedience?

Covenant Faith – Lesson Seven

The Transformation of Abram – Part 4

I. Abram Passes the Test of Strife

Genesis 13:6-9 (KJV)
[6] And the land was not able to bear them, that they might dwell together: for their substance was great, so that they could not dwell together. [7] And there was a strife between the herdmen of Abram's cattle and the herdmen of Lot's cattle: and the Canaanite and the Perizzite dwelled then in the land. [8] **And Abram said unto Lot, Let there be no strife, I pray thee, between me and thee, and between my herdmen and thy herdmen; for we *be* brethren**. [9] *Is* not the whole land before thee? separate thyself, I pray thee, from me: if *thou wilt take* the left hand, then I will go to the right; or if *thou depart* to the right hand, then I will go to the left.

Abram had returned again to the path that God had called him to. In our last lesson, we discovered that Abram came back out of Egypt and returned to the first place that he had met with God and had prepared an altar.   He was returning to the path that God had established for him.

The next test that he had to face in his journey to destiny was the test of strife. The Word has a lot to say about strife and how it should not be a part of the life of a believer. It also has a lot to say about living in the opposite of strife: the walk of love.

Notice that Abram lovingly presented a way NOT to walk with those in strife. One of the best things that he did was to separate himself from Lot and those in strife with his household.

II. The Love Walk

1 John 5:1-5 (KJV)
[1] Whosoever believeth that Jesus is the Christ is born of God: and every one that loveth him that begat loveth him also that is begotten of him. [2] By this we know that we love the children of God, when we love God, and keep his commandments. [3] For this is the love of God, that we keep his commandments: and his commandments are not grievous. [4] For whatsoever is born of God overcometh the world: and this is the victory that overcometh the world, *even* our faith. [5] Who is he that overcometh the world, but he that believeth that Jesus is the Son of God?

The Love Walk is the walk of victory for the life of the Believer. It is like a path that we follow. As long as we are on this path, our faith grows and we dwell in the protection of God. To step off this path is to step into Satan's territory.

To walk in love is not some wishie-washie lifestyle. The believer must:

- Love God
- Love Truth

- Love the Commandments of God
- Love the Judgments of God
- Love to See God's Will Accomplished on the Earth
- Love Spiritual Victory

Psalm 97:10 (KJV)
[10] Ye that love the LORD, hate evil: he preserveth the souls of his saints; he delivereth them out of the hand of the wicked.

- Hate Evil
- Hate Injustice
- Hate Darkness
- Hate Strife

Walking in the love of God and in His commandments is the pathway to victorious living!

III. Love is a Walk Without Strife

2 Timothy 2:22-26 (KJV)
[22] Flee also youthful lusts: but follow righteousness, faith, charity, peace, with them that call on the Lord out of a pure heart. [23] But foolish and unlearned questions avoid, knowing that they do gender strifes. [24] And the servant of the Lord must not strive; but be gentle unto all *men*, apt to teach, patient, [25] In meekness instructing those that oppose themselves; if God peradventure will give them repentance to the acknowledging of the truth; [26] And *that* they may recover themselves out of the snare of the devil, who are taken captive by him at his will.

The servant of God must be strife-free! He must walk in meekness. Those that walk in strife are haughty and lifted up in pride.

Those in strife are already taken captive by the devil. The only way that they can recover themselves is to repent of the pride and strife and yield in humility to God!

IV. Faith Works by Love

Galatians 5:6 (KJV)
[6] For in Jesus Christ neither circumcision availeth any thing, nor uncircumcision; **but faith which worketh by love**.

Worketh: Strongs # G **1754** ἐνεργέω energeo {en-erg-eh'-o} [10]
Meaning: 1) to be operative, be at work, put forth power 1a) to work for one, aid one 2) to effect 3) to display one's activity, show one's self operative.

This Greek word is where we get the words "energy" and "energize" from. When we walk in true biblical love, our faith is energized to move into the things of God. The opposite is also true: when we walk in strife, our faith is de-energized.

---

[10] Strong's Enhanced Lexicon. BibleWorks for Windows 7.0. BibleWorks, LLC, Norfolk, VA. Copyright © 2006.

V. Love Will Drive Out Fear

1 John 4:15-19 (KJV)

[15] Whosoever shall confess that Jesus is the Son of God, God dwelleth in him, and he in God. [16] And we have known and believed the love that God hath to us. God is love; and he that dwelleth in love dwelleth in God, and God in him. [17] Herein is our love made perfect, that we may have boldness in the day of judgment: because as he is, so are we in this world. [18] There is no fear in love; but perfect love casteth out fear: because fear hath torment. He that feareth is not made perfect in love. [19] We love him, because he first loved us.

When we walk in true biblical love, God is dwelling is us and we are dwelling in Him. In the dwelling with God, our love is made perfect.

Perfect: Strongs # G **<5048>** τελειόω (teleioo)[11]
Meaning: to bring to an end, to complete, perfect
Origin: from 5046
Usage: accomplish(2), accomplished(1), finish(1), fulfilled(1), made perfect(5), make perfect(2),perfect(2), perfected(7), reach a goal(1), spending the full number(1).

This word is derived from another word translated "perfect":

Strongs # G5046 τέλειος teleios {tel'-i-os} [12]
Meaning: 1) brought to its end, finished 2) wanting nothing necessary to completeness 3) perfect 4) that which is perfect 4a) consummate human integrity and virtue 4b) of men 4b1) full grown, adult, of full age, mature
Origin: from 5056; TDNT - 8:67,1161; adj
Usage: AV - perfect 17, man 1, of full age 1; 19

It is in the continual walking and dwelling with God that our love matures and becomes complete. When this biblical love has matured in us:

- It will drive out fear.
- It will give us boldness in the time of judgment!
- We will be like Jesus while in this world!

VI. Love Never Fails

1 Corinthians 13:8 (KJV)

[8] Charity never faileth: but whether *there be* prophecies, they shall fail; whether *there be* tongues, they shall cease; whether *there be* knowledge, it shall vanish away.

Love always continues. It will:

- Hold on to God's promises, when everyone else has given up.
- Hold on to God's commandments, when everyone else has abandoned them!

---

[11] Strong's Enhanced Lexicon. BibleWorks for Windows 7.0. BibleWorks, LLC, Norfolk, VA. Copyright © 2006.
[12] Strong's Enhanced Lexicon. BibleWorks for Windows 7.0. BibleWorks, LLC, Norfolk, VA. Copyright © 2006.

- Hold on to the knowledge of God's love for them, when everything around them seems to say the opposite.

Love will endure beyond prophecy, praying in tongues, and even knowledge itself!

VII. Learning to Be Moved by Love

Matthew 14:13-14 (KJV)
[13] When Jesus heard *of it*, he departed thence by ship into a desert place apart: and when the people had heard *thereof*, they followed him on foot out of the cities. [14] And Jesus went forth, and saw a great multitude, and was moved with compassion toward them, and he healed their sick.

Jesus had learned that His cousin, John, had been brutally murdered by Herod in a fit of lust for his step daughter. Jesus had every right to have responded in anger, and he could have stirred up a revolt against Herod. Instead, Jesus departed into a desert place to be alone with the Father. In the midst of this, Jesus saw the great multitude that needed Him. He was moved by love to go past His own hurt to meet their needs. Jesus knew the power of being moved with compassion.

We need to learn to respond to things in life from our spirit, because it is there that the love of God was placed by the Holy Spirit at the new birth.

Romans 5:5 (KJV)
[5] And hope maketh not ashamed; because the love of God is shed abroad in our hearts by the Holy Ghost which is given unto us.

VIII. Abram Passed the Test and His Vision was Expanded

Genesis 13:14-17 (KJV)
[14] And the LORD said unto Abram, after that Lot was separated from him, Lift up now thine eyes, and look from the place where thou art northward, and southward, and eastward, and westward: [15] For all the land which thou seest, to thee will I give it, and to thy seed for ever. [16] And I will make thy seed as the dust of the earth: so that if a man can number the dust of the earth, *then* shall thy seed also be numbered. [17] Arise, walk through the land in the length of it and in the breadth of it; for I will give it unto thee.

Because Abram rejected strife, his faith and vision were expanded by God.

Review Questions

1.   What is the next test to our development in covenant faith?

2.   What is the love walk?

3.   What does strife do?

4.   What does love do?

5.   How do we learn to be moved by love?

6.   What happens when we have passed the test of strife?

Covenant Faith – Lesson Eight

The Transformation of Abram – Part 5

I.   War in the Promised Land

In Genesis 17, we find that four kings had gathered their arms and fought against Sodom and Gomorrah. These kings prevailed and took everything: goods, men, women, children, and animals. They made one mistake: they took Lot and his family.

II.   Abram Becomes a Warrior

Genesis 14:11-16 (KJV)
[11] And they took all the goods of Sodom and Gomorrah, and all their victuals, and went their way. [12] And they took Lot, Abram's brother's son, who dwelt in Sodom, and his goods, and departed. [13] And there came one that had escaped, and told Abram the Hebrew; for he dwelt in the plain of Mamre the Amorite, brother of Eshcol, and brother of Aner: and these *were* confederate with Abram. [14] And when Abram heard that his brother was taken captive, he armed his trained *servants*, born in his own house, three hundred and eighteen, and pursued *them* unto Dan. [15] And he divided himself against them, he and his servants, by night, and smote them, and pursued them unto Hobah, which *is* on the left hand of Damascus. [16] And he brought back all the goods, and also brought again his brother Lot, and his goods, and the women also, and the people.

Abram had learned his lesson in Egypt. He allowed the blessing that God was building in his life to produce strength. He had trained those born within his own household to fight and protect.

Notice in verse thirteen:

"... these were confederate with Abram."

Abram and his household had gotten so strong that those in the area around him had aligned themselves with him.

Men and women of Covenant Faith will build up their ability to fight. They will prepare for battle and be ready when the enemy tries to encroach on their blessings from the hand of God.

The blessings of God are not to be squandered on pleasing the flesh; rather, they are to be used to build one's defenses and to prepare for the time of trouble!

Abram used strategic planning in making war. He used the cover of night and divided up his men to attack from several directions. Abram had won the battle and got everything back!

III. The Greatest Revelation in the Life of Abram

Genesis 14:18-20 (KJV)
[18] And <u>Melchizedek king of Salem brought forth bread and wine</u>: and he *was* the priest of the most high God. [19] And he blessed him, and said, Blessed *be* Abram of the most high God, possessor of heaven and earth: [20] And blessed be the most high God, which hath delivered thine enemies into thy hand. <u>And he gave him tithes of all</u>.

There is much mystery regarding Melchizedek. We find in the Book of Hebrews:

Hebrews 7:1-4 (KJV)
[1] For this Melchisedec, king of Salem, priest of the most high God, who met Abraham returning from the slaughter of the kings, and blessed him; [2] To whom also Abraham gave a tenth part of all; first being by interpretation King of righteousness, and after that also King of Salem, which is, King of peace; [3] Without father, without mother, without descent, having neither beginning of days, nor end of life; but made like unto the Son of God; abideth a priest continually. [4] Now consider how great this man *was*, unto whom even the patriarch Abraham gave the tenth of the spoils.

Melchizedek means "King of Righteousness." Most likely, this was his title rather than his name. It is very likely that this was a Christophanies: the pre-incarnate Christ appearing in the Old Testament to give Abram the greatest revelation he would ever receive: the mystery of the Bread and Wine. I believe that Jesus gave communion to Abram and explained to him God's plan!

The greatest revelations that we will ever receive, many times, will be after the battle is won. We have taken what God has given to us, strengthened ourselves, and prepared to fight. When we raise up in our current position and manifest a level of victory that the blessing was to establish, God always gives us a greater revelation.

This concept of bread and wine is incorporated in two places among the Hebrews:

1.   **The Beginning of Ev' Shabbat**: This reveals that the Sabbath is a divine rehearsal of the Millennial Reign of Messiah.

2.   **The Passover Meal**: In the Passover meal, there are three pieces of mitzvah representing Abraham, Isaac and Jacob. It is the second piece of mitzvah that is broken. Isaac was the son of Promise and Abraham was willing to offer him up on the altar for God. This opened the door for God the Father to offer up His Son on the altar of the Cross for mankind!

Abram's response to this revelation was to give the tithe of all he had to Melchizedek. From this point on, the tithe is forever connected to the instruction in the ways and purposes of God!

IV. Abram Rejects Carnal Reward

Genesis 14:21-24 (KJV)

[21] And the king of Sodom said unto Abram, Give me the persons, and take the goods to thyself. [22] And Abram said to the king of Sodom, I have lift up mine hand unto the LORD, the most high God, the possessor of heaven and earth, [23] That I will not *take* from a thread even to a shoelatchet, and that I will not take any thing that *is* thine, lest thou shouldest say, I have made Abram rich: [24] Save only that which the young men have eaten, and the portion of the men which went with me, Aner, Eshcol, and Mamre; let them take their portion.

Today's preachers would have taken the gifts from the king of Sodom and preached about how quickly they got a return on their tithe! How far we have fallen from the example of Abram!

Abram knew is his heart what God was going to do in his life. He did not want such a sinful man as the king of Sodom taking credit for any of the blessings God was establishing in him.

Abram did allow the men that fought with him to take their portion.

Review Questions

1.   What did Abram do with the blessings God gave him?

2.   When did the greatest revelation Abram ever received come?

3.   What was this great revelation?

_____
_____
_____
_____
_____
_____

4.   Where was this revelation embedded in our Hebraic heritage?

_____
_____
_____
_____
_____
_____
_____
_____

Covenant Faith – Lesson Nine

The Transformation of Abram – Part 6

I.   Abram Passes the Test of Worldly Riches

We ended our last lesson with the fact that Abram refused the wealth of Sodom. This is another pivotal point in his life. The world would tell us that he deserved the wealth of Sodom because of his conquest. Remember, the wealth was enough that four kings fought to get it! Yet we find Abram refusing it.

Satan will always tempt us to gain wealth through compromise with the world. Even when we do something that blesses the world, the world will try to reward it with riches that include strings of compromise. Accept wealth on their terms and they will end up calling in favors and pulling your strings the rest of your life.

Because Abram passed this secondary test (the first was warfare), God comes to him in Chapter 15 and expands his understanding of his relationship with God and God's promises to him.

II.   God Expands Abram's Understanding

Genesis 15:1 (KJV)
[1] After these things the word of the LORD came unto Abram in a vision, saying, Fear not, Abram: I *am* thy shield, *and* thy exceeding great reward.

God comes to Abram in a dream and tells him several things:

1.   **The reason you did so well in battle is that I am your shield**. God is the ultimate force field of protection. The protection of God is one of the greatest benefits a believer can have.

2.   **I am your exceeding great reward**. What a statement! God was basically telling Abram: "You turned down the filthy wealth of Sodom, so now I am your exceeding great reward." I will take God over worldly wealth any day!

Genesis 15:2-3 (KJV)
[2] And Abram said, Lord GOD, what wilt thou give me, seeing I go childless, and the steward of my house *is* this Eliezer of Damascus? [3] And Abram said, Behold, to me thou hast given no seed: and, lo, one born in my house is mine heir.

After the revelation that Melchizedek gave him regarding the bread and wine, Abram is ready to move forward with producing his heir. In his heart, he now knows what God is wanting and desires to move forward.

Genesis 15:4-6 (KJV)
[4] And, behold, the word of the LORD *came* unto him, saying, This shall not be thine heir; but he that shall come forth out of thine own bowels shall be thine heir. [5] And he brought him forth abroad, and said, Look now toward heaven, and tell the stars, if thou

be able to number them: and he said unto him, So shall thy seed be. [6] And he believed in the LORD; and he counted it to him for righteousness.

God begins to define, refine, and expand Abram's understanding.

His Seed: Abram, the promise is going to be your seed. What I am doing in your heart is so great, it cannot help but produce!

His Vision: Look at all the stars in the heavens. Try your best to number them. That is how many descendants you will eventually have!

His Faith: Right here is where we establish the pattern of entering into what God and Abram would do. Abram believed God when it looked impossible.

> **Romans 4:16-22 (KJV)**
> [16] Therefore *it is* of faith, that *it might be* by grace; to the end the promise might be sure to all the seed; not to that only which is of the law, but to that also which is of the faith of Abraham; who is the father of us all, [17] (As it is written, I have made thee a father of many nations,) before him whom he believed, *even* God, who quickeneth the dead, and calleth those things which be not as though they were. [18] Who against hope believed in hope, that he might become the father of many nations, according to that which was spoken, So shall thy seed be. [19] And being not weak in faith, he considered not his own body now dead, when he was about an hundred years old, neither yet the deadness of Sara's womb: [20] He staggered not at the promise of God through unbelief; but was strong in faith, giving glory to God; [21] And being fully persuaded that, what he had promised, he was able also to perform. [22] And therefore it was imputed to him for righteousness.

III. The Power of Covenant

> **Genesis 15:7-18 (KJV)**
> [7] And he said unto him, I *am* the LORD that brought thee out of Ur of the Chaldees, to give thee this land to inherit it. [8] And he said, Lord GOD, whereby shall I know that I shall inherit it? [9] And he said unto him, Take me an heifer of three years old, and a she goat of three years old, and a ram of three years old, and a turtledove, and a young pigeon. [10] And he took unto him all these, and divided them in the midst, and laid each piece one against another: but the birds divided he not. [11] And when the fowls came down upon the carcases, Abram drove them away. [12] And when the sun was going down, a deep sleep fell upon Abram; and, lo, an horror of great darkness fell upon him. [13] And he said unto Abram, Know of a surety that thy seed shall be a stranger in a land *that is* not theirs, and shall serve them; and they shall afflict them four hundred years; [14] And also that nation, whom they shall serve, will I judge: and afterward shall they come out with great substance. [15] And thou shalt go to thy fathers in peace; thou shalt be buried in a good old age. [16] But in the fourth generation they shall come hither again: for the iniquity of the Amorites *is* not yet full. [17] And it came to pass, that, when the sun went down, and it was dark, behold a smoking furnace, and a burning lamp that passed between those pieces. [18] In the same day the LORD made a covenant with Abram . . .

God is now ready to cut a covenant with Abram. Before this event, Abram only had promises. This is God becoming Abram's exceeding great reward: God was entering into blood covenant with Abram.

I want you to notice several important things about this event:

> [11] And when the fowls came down upon the carcases, Abram drove them away.

Right before moving from promise to covenant is a precarious time. The covenant must be protected until it is ratified. Satan sent the fowl of the air to try to desecrate the sacrifice needed for the covenant. Abram stood guard to keep the sacrifice intact.

Today some of the fowl of the air are manifested in pulpits, seminaries and universities. They seek to water down the power of the Cross and the sacrifice Jesus made for us. We are the ones that are responsible to protect the truth: first in our own hearts and then in society around us.

> [13] And he said unto Abram, Know of a surety that thy seed shall be a stranger in a land *that is* not theirs, and shall serve them; and they shall afflict them four hundred years; [14] And also that nation, whom they shall serve, will I judge: and afterward shall they come out with great substance.

God now gives full disclosure to Abram about his children going into Egypt, their slavery there, and their coming out with great wealth. (Remember, Abram had established the pattern!)

> [15] And thou shalt go to thy fathers in peace; thou shalt be buried in a good old age.

God gives the revelation of a long and peaceful life.

> [16] But in the fourth generation they shall come hither again: for the iniquity of the Amorites *is* not yet full.

For the iniquity of the Amorites is not yet full. God would use the expanded descendants of Abram to eventually judge the Amorites: when their iniquity was full. God will never judge anything before its time. Once iniquity is full within a people, Heaven will always respond!

> [17] And it came to pass, that, when the sun went down, and it was dark, behold a smoking furnace, and a burning lamp that passed between those pieces. [18] In the same day the LORD made a covenant with Abram . . .

This covenant was established by both God the Father (the smoking furnace) and God the Son (a burning lamp). This covenant was not only between God and Abram, but God the Father and God the Son (to whom the promise was made – Jesus was the Seed!)

This is why if we stumble, the One who holds the promise can forgive and re-establish us!

Review Questions

1.   Why can the place of victory be the most dangerous place for us?

_____
_____
_____
_____
_____
_____
_____
_____

2.   What were the two initial expansions in Abram's understanding of God?

_____
_____
_____
_____
_____
_____
_____
_____
_____

3.   God also defined, refined, and expanded Abram's understanding in three key areas. Expound on each:

His Seed:
_____
_____
_____
_____

His Vision:
_____
_____
_____

His Faith:
_____
_____
_____

4.   When you move from promise to covenant, it is such a precarious time. Why?

Covenant Faith – Lesson Ten

The Transformation of Abram – Part 7

I.   Impatience and God's Promise

Genesis 16:1-3 (KJV)
[1] Now Sarai Abram's wife bare him no children: and she had an handmaid, an Egyptian, whose name *was* Hagar. [2] And Sarai said unto Abram, Behold now, the LORD hath restrained me from bearing: I pray thee, go in unto my maid; it may be that I may obtain children by her. And Abram hearkened to the voice of Sarai. [3] And Sarai Abram's wife took Hagar her maid the Egyptian, after Abram had dwelt ten years in the land of Canaan, and gave her to her husband Abram to be his wife.

One of the things that both Abram and Sarai suffered from was impatience with God. God has promised them a son, but the delay was hard to handle. First, Abram suggested that the son of his faithful servant and friend become that child, and then Sarai suggested that Abram sleep with her handmaid!

Both of these ideas seem hair-brained to us in the twenty-first century – especially Sarai's idea! We need to realize that neither one of them originated the ideas. These were the customs of the land they were from. Although God had gotten their bodies out of Babylon, segments of Babylon were still firmly seated within their minds.

They are guilty of the same thing we are: we do not examine our underlining assumptions and beliefs that operate at the subconscious level and examine them by God's ways. That is where we all get into trouble!

There are elements we have accepted at the base level of our belief systems that are drawn from the culture in which we were raised. These beliefs are contrary to the ways of God. Unless we examine them, they will come up when we are stressed and get us into trouble!

II.   Abram Harkened to Sarai!

". . . And Abram hearkened to the voice of Sarai."

This is a sticking point in this narrative. Abram will be corrected on this later by God.

Again, both Abram and Sarai were following the customs of their land. It was the woman that must decide to offer her handmaiden. She must initiate the process, and she brought Hagar into Abram. They both did everything according to protocol . . . the protocol of Babylon!

III.   Trouble in the Family

Genesis 16:4-6 (KJV)
[4] And he went in unto Hagar, and she conceived: and when she saw that she had conceived, her mistress was despised in her eyes. [5] And Sarai said unto Abram, My wrong *be* upon thee: I have given my maid into thy bosom; and when she saw that she had conceived, I was despised in her eyes: the LORD judge between me and thee. [6] But Abram said unto Sarai, Behold, thy maid *is* in thy hand; do to her as it pleaseth thee. And when Sarai dealt hardly with her, she fled from her face.

As soon as Hagar conceived, she despised Sarai. This happens when you try to do something for the Kingdom by a cultural protocol that was not of God!

Sarai said all of the blame for this situation was Abram's.

Abram basically told Sarai: "This was your idea, so you do what you want about it."

IV.   Divine Intervention

Hagar runs away and an angel appears unto her. The God of Abram hears her cry. That is what the name "Ishmael" means. Because he was from the loins of Abram, he was blessed by God.

V.   God Corrects Abram and Takes Him to the Next Level

Genesis 17:1-6 (KJV)
[1] And when Abram was ninety years old and nine, the LORD appeared to Abram, and said unto him, I *am* the Almighty God; walk before me, and be thou perfect. [2] And I will make my covenant between me and thee, and will multiply thee exceedingly. [3] And Abram fell on his face: and God talked with him, saying, [4] As for me, behold, my covenant *is* with thee, and thou shalt be a father of many nations. [5] Neither shall thy name any more be called Abram, but thy name shall be Abraham; for a father of many nations have I made thee. [6] And I will make thee exceeding fruitful, and I will make nations of thee, and kings shall come out of thee.

Notes from the New Pilgrim Study Bible

"In Hebrew El (the strong One) Shaddai (the breasted One). Abraham now learns that God is not only El, the strong mighty Creator who can do wonders, but the One who cares for him as a mother would, for He is the all-sufficient One. As mothers do, El Shaddai reproves Abraham for obeying someone else. Abraham had followed Sarah's advice instead of 'walking before' God only."[13]

You cannot fulfill what God has promised to you by the cultural traditions around you nor on the advice of others. It must come from the mind and the hand of God!

---

[13] The New Pilgrim Bible KJV Student Edition. Oxford University Press, Oxford, NY. © Copyright 1948, 1976, 2003. Page 30.

Walk Before Me and Be Perfect

Walk: Strongs # H **1980** הָלַךְ halak {haw-lak'} [14]

Meaning: 1) to go, walk, come 1a) (Qal) 1a1) to go, walk, come, depart, proceed, move, go away 1a2) to die, live, manner of life (fig.) 1b) (Piel) 1b1) to walk 1b2) to walk (fig.) 1c) (Hithpael) 1c1) to traverse 1c2) to walk about 1d) (Niphal) to lead, bring, lead away, carry, cause to walk
Origin: akin to 03212, a primitive root; TWOT - 498; v
Usage: AV - go 217, walk 156, come 16, ...away 7, ...along 6, misc 98; 500

Before Me: Strongs # H **6440** פָּנִים paniym {paw-neem'} pl. [15]

Meaning: 1) face 1a) face, faces 1b) presence, person 1c) face (of seraphim or cherubim) 1d) face (of animals) 1e) face, surface (of ground) 1f) as adv of loc/temp 1f1) before and behind, toward, in front of, forward, formerly, from beforetime, before 1g) with prep 1g1) in front of, before, to the front of, in the presence of, in the face of, at the face or front of, from the presence of, from before, from before the face of
Origin: from 06437; TWOT - 1782a; n m
Usage: AV - before 1137, face 390, presence 76, because 67, sight 40, countenance 30, from 27, person 21, upon 20, of 20, ...me 18, against 17, ...him 16, open 13, for 13, toward 9, misc 195; 2109

Perfect: Strongs # H8549 תָּמִים tamiym {taw-meem'}[16]

Meaning: 1) complete, whole, entire, sound 1a) complete, whole, entire 1b) whole, sound, healthful 1c) complete, entire (of time) 1d) sound, wholesome, unimpaired, innocent, having integrity 1e) what is complete or entirely in accord with truth and fact (neuter adj/subst)
Origin: from 08552; TWOT - 2522d; adj
Usage: AV - without blemish 44, perfect 18, upright 8, without spot 6, uprightly 4, whole 4, sincerely 2, complete 1, full 1, misc 3; 91

I now want you to walk with Me. As you do, I will make you entire, complete, and sound!

When Abram stopped visiting with God and started walking continually with God, then and only then, did he become Abraham!

[14] Strong's Enhanced Lexicon. BibleWorks for Windows 7.0. BibleWorks, LLC, Norfolk, VA. Copyright © 2006.
[15] Strong's Enhanced Lexicon. BibleWorks for Windows 7.0. BibleWorks, LLC, Norfolk, VA. Copyright © 2006.
[16] Strong's Enhanced Lexicon. BibleWorks for Windows 7.0. BibleWorks, LLC, Norfolk, VA. Copyright © 2006.

Review Questions

1. How can our traditions and culture get in the way of God's promises?

2. What does fleshly fulfillment do with the spiritual fulfillment of God's promise?

3. Describe in your own words what "halak paniym tamiym" means.

Covenant Faith – Lesson Eleven

The Faithful Intercessor

I. Inviting God In

Genesis 18:1-3 (KJV)
[1] And the LORD appeared unto him in the plains of Mamre: and he sat in the tent door in the heat of the day; [2] And he lift up his eyes and looked, and, lo, three men stood by him: and when he saw *them*, he ran to meet them from the tent door, and bowed himself toward the ground, [3] And said, My Lord, if now I have found favour in thy sight, pass not away, I pray thee, from thy servant:

In prior times in the life of Abraham, God would simply show up and make the meeting between Him and Abraham happen. Now that Abraham has entered a new level in his relationship with God, it would appear that God was on the way to doing something and would have passed right by, if Abraham had not pleaded for Him to stay awhile.

During some of the most strategic times spiritually in our lives, we must take the initiative to invite God in. If we do not, God will continue on and we will miss an important opportunity.

Jesus Would Have Passed By

Mark 6:45-50 (KJV)
[45] And straightway he constrained his disciples to get into the ship, and to go to the other side before unto Bethsaida, while he sent away the people. [46] And when he had sent them away, he departed into a mountain to pray. [47] And when even was come, the ship was in the midst of the sea, and he alone on the land. [48] And he saw them toiling in rowing; for the wind was contrary unto them: and about the fourth watch of the night he cometh unto them, walking upon the sea, and would have passed by them. [49] But when they saw him walking upon the sea, they supposed it had been a spirit, and cried out: [50] For they all saw him, and were troubled. And immediately he talked with them, and saith unto them, Be of good cheer: it is I; be not afraid.

Here we find Jesus walking on the water. Mark stressed that He would have passed on by them if they had not cried out!

II. Abraham Made God Feel Welcome

Genesis 18:3-8 (KJV)
[3] And said, My Lord, if now I have found favour in thy sight, pass not away, I pray thee, from thy servant: [4] Let a little water, I pray you, be fetched, and wash your feet, and rest yourselves under the tree: [5] And I will fetch a morsel of bread, and comfort ye your hearts; after that ye shall pass on: for therefore are ye come to your servant. And they said, So do, as thou hast said. [6] And Abraham hastened into the tent unto Sarah, and said, Make ready quickly three measures of fine meal, knead *it*, and make cakes upon the hearth. [7] And Abraham ran unto the herd, and

fetcht a calf tender and good, and gave *it* unto a young man; and he hasted to dress it. [8] And he took butter, and milk, and the calf which he had dressed, and set *it* before them; and he stood by them under the tree, and they did eat.

Abraham asks the men to rest, allow their feet to be washed, and to get a little bit to eat. Once they accepted, he went all out and prepared a full meal to include cooking a calf. It was like inviting someone for a quick sandwich and then preparing a Thanksgiving meal!

When was the last time that we went all out to prepare something for God? We need to make God's presence important in our lives and go out of our way to make Him feel special!

III.   Is Any Thing Too Hard for the LORD?

Genesis 18:9-15 (KJV)
[9] And they said unto him, Where *is* Sarah thy wife? And he said, Behold, in the tent. [10] And he said, I will certainly return unto thee according to the time of life; and, lo, Sarah thy wife shall have a son. And Sarah heard *it* in the tent door, which *was* behind him. [11] Now Abraham and Sarah *were* old *and* well stricken in age; *and* it ceased to be with Sarah after the manner of women. [12] Therefore Sarah laughed within herself, saying, After I am waxed old shall I have pleasure, my lord being old also? [13] And the LORD said unto Abraham, Wherefore did Sarah laugh, saying, Shall I of a surety bear a child, which am old? [14] Is any thing too hard for the LORD? At the time appointed I will return unto thee, according to the time of life, and Sarah shall have a son. [15] Then Sarah denied, saying, I laughed not; for she was afraid. And he said, Nay; but thou didst laugh.

Sometimes God delays things so that He alone will get the glory. We need to respond in faith to the "is anything too hard for the LORD?" in our lives. We are dealing with the Almighty that spoke and the universe became! How difficult is it really for Him to do what He has promised compared to what He has already done?

IV.   Abraham the Intercessor

Genesis 18:16-22 (KJV)
[16] And the men rose up from thence, and looked toward Sodom: and Abraham went with them to bring them on the way. [17] And the LORD said, Shall I hide from Abraham that thing which I do; [18] Seeing that Abraham shall surely become a great and mighty nation, and all the nations of the earth shall be blessed in him? [19] For I know him, that he will command his children and his household after him, and they shall keep the way of the LORD, to do justice and judgment; that the LORD may bring upon Abraham that which he hath spoken of him. [20] And the LORD said, Because the cry of Sodom and Gomorrah is great, and because their sin is very grievous; [21] I will go down now, and see whether they have done altogether according to the cry of it, which is come unto me; and if not, I will know. [22] And the men turned their faces from thence, and went toward Sodom: but Abraham stood yet before the LORD.

Before we get into the intercession of Abraham, I want you to notice what God said about him. He will command his children and household to:

- Keep the way of God.
- To do justice.
- To do Judgment.

Justice: Strongs #H 6666 צְדָקָה tsedaqah {tsed-aw-kaw'} [17]

Meaning: 1) justice, righteousness 1a) righteousness (in government) 1a1) of judge, ruler, king 1a2) of law 1a3) of Davidic king Messiah 1b) righteousness (of God's attribute) 1c) righteousness (in a case or cause) 1d) righteousness, truthfulness 1e) righteousness (as ethically right) 1f) righteousness (as vindicated), justification, salvation 1f1) of God 1f2) prosperity (of people) 1g) righteous acts
Origin: from 06663; TWOT - 1879b; n f
Usage: AV - righteousness 128, justice 15, right 9, righteous acts 3, moderately 1, righteously 1; 157

Judgment: Strongs #H 4941 מִשְׁפָּט mishpat {mish-pawt'} [18]

Meaning: 1) judgment, justice, ordinance 1a) judgment 1a1) act of deciding a case 1a2) place, court, seat of judgment 1a3) process, procedure, litigation (before judges) 1a4) case, cause (presented for judgment) 1a5) sentence, decision (of judgment) 1a6) execution (of judgment) 1a7) time (of judgment) 1b) justice, right, rectitude (attributes of God or man) 1c) ordinance 1d) decision (in law) 1e) right, privilege, due (legal) 1f) proper, fitting, measure, fitness, custom, manner, plan
Origin: from 08199; TWOT - 2443c; n m
Usage: AV - judgment 296, manner 38, right 18, cause 12, ordinance 11, lawful 7, order 5, worthy 3, fashion 3, custom 2, discretion 2, law 2, measure 2, sentence 2, misc 18; 421

I think that sometimes we miss what God said about Abraham. He would walk in righteousness and sit as a judge through intercession. We have been grafted into this great legacy!

". . . but Abraham Stood Before the LORD."

God had set His face toward Sodom and Gomorrah, but Abraham positioned himself between God and the twin cities. This is the job of the intercessor.

Ezekiel 22:23-31 (KJV)

[23] And the word of the LORD came unto me, saying, [24] Son of man, say unto her, Thou *art* the land that is not cleansed, nor rained upon in the day of indignation. [25] *There is* a conspiracy of her prophets in the midst thereof, like a roaring lion ravening the prey; they have devoured souls; they have taken the treasure and precious things; they have made her many widows in the midst thereof. [26] Her priests have violated my law, and have profaned mine holy things: they have put no difference between the holy and profane, neither have they shewed *difference* between the unclean and the clean, and have hid their eyes from my sabbaths, and I am profaned among them. [27] Her princes in the midst thereof *are* like wolves ravening the prey, to shed blood, *and* to destroy souls, to get dishonest gain. [28] And her prophets have daubed them with untempered *morter*, seeing vanity, and divining lies unto them, saying, Thus saith the Lord GOD, when the LORD hath not spoken. [29] The people of the land have used oppression, and exercised robbery, and have vexed the poor and needy: yea, they have oppressed the stranger

---

[17] Strong's Enhanced Lexicon. BibleWorks for Windows 7.0. BibleWorks, LLC, Norfolk, VA. Copyright © 2006.
[18] Strong's Enhanced Lexicon. BibleWorks for Windows 7.0. BibleWorks, LLC, Norfolk, VA. Copyright © 2006.

wrongfully. ³⁰ <u>And I sought for a man among them, that should make up the hedge, and stand in the gap before me for the land, that I should not destroy it: but I found none</u>. ³¹ Therefore have I poured out mine indignation upon them; I have consumed them with the fire of my wrath: their own way have I recompensed upon their heads, saith the Lord GOD.

Within the past month, I have provided copies of the videos from Lindsay Williams to many so that we might intercede and prepare. America has become a Sodom and Gomorrah is so many ways. God is walking by His people to see who will go out of their way to invite Him in. He is waiting for the children of Abraham to stand between Him and America.

We need to remember that the Elite are not gods (although they think they are headed in that direction). They are no more gods than Nebuchadnezzar of Babylon was. This pagan was called "God's servant" used to judge God's people – nothing more. The Elite are the same way. They will only get done what God allows them to accomplish. The Almighty has forced them, time and time again, to adjust their plans. Where are the children of Abraham that will stand between God and America to intercede?

If America goes down, it will be because the Church has lost the calling of Abraham to:

- Keep the way of God.
- To do justice.
- To do judgment.

Review Questions

1. Why is it significant that Abraham invited God in to rest and to eat with him?

2. What empowered Abraham's Intercession?

3.   What is so significant when the scripture says, "but Abraham stood before the LORD"?

Covenant Faith – Lesson Twelve

God's Covenant Man Opens the Door to Salvation

I.   Abraham's Final Exam Has Come

Genesis 22:1-2 (KJV)

[1] And it came to pass after these things, that God did tempt Abraham, and said unto him, Abraham: and he said, Behold, *here* I *am*. [2] And he said, Take now thy son, thine only *son* Isaac, whom thou lovest, and get thee into the land of Moriah; and offer him there for a burnt offering upon one of the mountains which I will tell thee of.

Tempt: Strongs #H **5254** נָסָה nacah {naw-saw'} [19]

Meaning: 1) to test, try, prove, tempt, assay, put to the proof or test 1a) (Piel) 1a1) to test, try 1a2) to attempt, assay, try 1a3) to test, try, prove, tempt

Origin: a primitive root; TWOT - 1373; v

Usage: AV - prove 20, tempt 12, assay 2, adventure 1, try 1; 36

Abraham had grown to the place spiritually where his final exam in the Kingdom had come. We need to also realize that although the KJV translates **nacah** as "tempt," it is more accurately translated as "test" or "prove." This is important to understand. The Word tells us:

James 1:13 (KJV)

[13] Let no man say when he is tempted, I am tempted of God: for God cannot be tempted with evil, neither tempteth he any man:

God was not tempting Abraham to sin here in Genesis 22. I prefer the military term for testing new advanced weapons: prove. In military proving grounds, advanced weapons are tested under extreme conditions to ascertain their accuracy and reliability. We need to understand that the "proving" of Abraham was a spiritual weapon of untold devastating power against the Kingdom of Darkness. We will deal more on this divine weapon later on in this lesson.

God instructs Abraham to take his only son (i.e. the son of promise) to Mount Moriah and to offer him as a sacrifice to the LORD. Abraham did not argue or protest: he moved in faith and the knowledge of what Melchizedek gave him with the bread and wine.

II.   Third Day Principle

Genesis 22:3-5 (KJV)

[3] And Abraham rose up early in the morning, and saddled his ass, and took two of his young men with him, and Isaac his son, and clave the wood for the burnt offering, and rose up, and went unto the place of which God had told him. [4] Then on the third day Abraham lifted up his eyes, and saw the place afar off. [5] And Abraham said unto his young men, Abide ye here with the ass; and I and the lad will go yonder and worship, and come again to you.

---

[19] Strong's Enhanced Lexicon. BibleWorks for Windows 7.0. BibleWorks, LLC, Norfolk, VA. Copyright © 2006.

I want you to notice several things about these verses:

1.   It was on the third day of the journey that he lifted up his eyes and saw the place. God had encoded resurrection into the journey!

2.   "I and the lad will go yonder and worship, and come again to you." This is faith speaking! Abraham's language expressed that they both would go up and that they both would come back down!

The Vision of Abraham

Hebrews 11:17-19 (KJV)
[17] By faith Abraham, when he was tried, offered up Isaac: and he that had received the promises offered up his only begotten *son*, [18] Of whom it was said, That in Isaac shall thy seed be called: [19] Accounting that God *was* able to raise *him* up, even from the dead; from whence also he received him in a figure.

Before there was ever a resurrection on the earth, Abraham believed that God would raise Isaac back from the ashes to life again.

III.   God Will Provide a Lamb!

Genesis 22:6-8 (KJV)
[6] And Abraham took the wood of the burnt offering, and laid *it* upon Isaac his son; and he took the fire in his hand, and a knife; and they went both of them together. [7] And Isaac spake unto Abraham his father, and said, My father: and he said, Here *am* I, my son. And he said, Behold the fire and the wood: but where *is* the lamb for a burnt offering? [8] And Abraham said, My son, God will provide himself a lamb for a burnt offering: so they went both of them together.

God will provide Himself a lamb! As Abraham moved in obedience to God, the prophetic anointing began to flow in him. These prophetic words would burn within Hebraic consciousness for over two thousand years!

IV.   Abraham's Test

Genesis 22:9-11 (KJV)
[9] And they came to the place which God had told him of; and Abraham built an altar there, and laid the wood in order, and bound Isaac his son, and laid him on the altar upon the wood. [10] And Abraham stretched forth his hand, and took the knife to slay his son. [11] And the angel of the LORD called unto him out of heaven, and said, Abraham, Abraham: and he said, Here *am* I.

In obedience, Abraham bound up Isaac and was ready to offer him up as a sacrifice to God. He was fully prepared to move completely in obedience. Only God could stop him!

Abraham was "willing" to obey. We do not understand the power of being "willing." There are times that God may ask us to do the unimaginable to see if "willing" was in our hearts. Many times, all He requires is "willing" and not the follow through. "Willing" must always be added to faith to receive His blessing!

Isaiah 1:19 (KJV)
[19] If ye be willing and obedient, ye shall eat the good of the land:

V.   God Provides

Genesis 22:12-14 (KJV)
[12] And he said, Lay not thine hand upon the lad, neither do thou any thing unto him: for now I know that thou fearest God, seeing thou hast not withheld thy son, thine only *son* from me. [13] And Abraham lifted up his eyes, and looked, and behold behind *him* a ram caught in a thicket by his horns: and Abraham went and took the ram, and offered him up for a burnt offering in the stead of his son. [14] And Abraham called the name of that place Jehovah-jireh: as it is said *to* this day, In the mount of the LORD it shall be seen.

Notice in this story that God did not provide a lamb at that time; He provided a ram. The Lamb of God would not show up for about two thousand years. All that time, every Hebrew and every Rabbi, were looking for the lamb that God would provide. That expectation was fulfilled one day as the prophet cried:

John 1:29 (KJV)
[29] The next day John seeth Jesus coming unto him, and saith, Behold the Lamb of God, which taketh away the sin of the world.

The spiritual weapon that was tested in Abraham hit its target on the shores of Galilee!

God's covenant man (Abraham) was willing to sacrifice his only begotten son of promise for God. This watershed event then allowed God to offer His only begotten Son upon the altar of the Cross for mankind! I want you to see the accuracy of God's weaponry. Abraham was going to offer Isaac on Mount Moriah to God and Jesus was offered up for us on the very same spot! Mount Morah became part of Jerusalem!!

Jehovah-Jireh

It is amazing how modern Christianity makes everything about money. We are certainly in the Laodicean age!   I do not find money anywhere in these verses. But I do see God providing what gold and silver cannot: salvation!

VI. The Blessing Flows

Genesis 22:15-18 (KJV)
[15] And the angel of the LORD called unto Abraham out of heaven the second time, [16] And said, By myself have I sworn, saith the LORD, for because thou hast done this thing, and hast not withheld thy son, thine only *son*: [17] That in blessing I will bless thee, and in multiplying I will multiply thy seed as the stars of the heaven, and as the sand which *is* upon the sea shore; and thy seed shall possess the gate of his enemies; [18] And in thy seed shall all the nations of the earth be blessed; because thou hast obeyed my voice.

"...because thou hast obeyed my voice." What a powerful statement, and it is the key to real blessing from God: obedience!

"...and thy seed shall possess the gates of his enemies." Remember what Jesus said:

Matthew 16:18 (KJV)
[18] And I say also unto thee, That thou art Peter, and upon this rock I will build my church; and the gates of hell shall not prevail against it.

Upon the rock of revelation that Jesus was the Lamb of God, Messiah, and the Seed, He would build His church. If the gates of hell cannot prevail against it, then the Seed will possess the gates!

Review Questions

1. What is the difference between "tempting" and "testing"?

2. How is the resurrection encoded into the story?

3.   What did Abraham establish in the passing of this test?

_____
_____
_____
_____
_____
_____
_____
_____
_____

Covenant Faith – Lesson Thirteen

Developing Covenant Faith – Part 1

I.   The Two Sides of the Coin of Faith

Constantly Being Faithful to Our Covenant with God	Constantly Believing God Over the World and Its System Around Us

For most today, the teaching of faith is reduced down to standing on God's promises to get what you want in life and to overcome the bad circumstances that life can throw at you. Although there is great power in the promises of God, without teaching on our responsibilities to God, faith can be reduced to a new age type of teaching to fulfill the desires of the flesh! So, in this lesson, we will be examining how to develop in both areas to keep balanced.

II.   The Just Shall Live By Faith

Romans 1:16-18 (KJV)
[16] For I am not ashamed of the gospel of Christ: for it is the power of God unto salvation to every one that believeth; to the Jew first, and also to the Greek. [17] For therein is the righteousness of God revealed from faith to faith: as it is written, <u>The just shall live by faith.</u> [18] <u>For the wrath of God is revealed from heaven against all ungodliness and unrighteousness of men, who hold the truth in unrighteousness</u>;

There are several things that we need to look at in these powerful verses:

1. **The Gospel is the Power of God.**

In our day, the only way to tap into the power of God is in the Gospel! If there are those that seem to have power, but not the Gospel of the death, burial, and resurrection of Jesus, the power that they are moving in is not of God.

2. **The Just Shall Live by Faith.**

This is more than just standing on the promises of God. Paul is quoting Hab. 2:4.

Habakkuk 2:1-4 (KJV)
[1] I will stand upon my watch, and set me upon the tower, and will watch to see what he will say unto me, and what I shall answer when I am reproved. [2] And the LORD answered me, and said, Write the vision, and make *it* plain upon tables, that he may run that readeth it. [3] For the vision *is* yet for an appointed time, but at the end it shall speak, and not lie: though it tarry, wait for it; because it will surely come, it will not tarry. [4] Behold, his soul *which* is lifted up is not upright in him: <u>but the just shall live by his faith.</u>

Shall Live by Faith

Faith: Strongs # H **0530** אֱמוּנָה 'emuwnah {em-oo-naw') or (shortened) אֱמֻנָה 'emunah {em-oo-naw'} [20]
Meaning: 1) firmness, fidelity, steadfastness, steadiness
Origin: from 0529; TWOT - 116e; n f
Usage: AV - faithfulness 18, truth 13, faithfully 5, office 5, faithful 3, faith 1, stability 1, steady 1, truly 1, verily 1; 49
There are no notes for this verse.

When we look at the original Hebrew in this verse, we get a different picture from what is being taught today. This man is not living on the promises of God; rather, he is living by the requirements of God: commandments, statutes, and judgments. He is steadfastly walking in them with firmness and fidelity! This keeps him from becoming the man in verse 5 and beyond.

The Lifted Up and Not Upright Man

Habakkuk goes on in verse 5 to tell about the one who is lifted up and is not upright. Finis Dake makes these comments on this man:

Notes for Verse 5[21]
[**He is a proud man**] Twelve Facts about the Self-Exalted Man:

1.   He is not upright (Hab. 2:4).
2.   He does not live by faith.
3.   He is a wine drinker (Hab. 2:5).
4.   He is proud.
5.   He roams idly from home.
6.   He enlarges his desire as hell (Hades).
7.   He is like death that cannot be satisfied.
8.   He is greedy (Hab. 2:6).
9.   He is covetous (Hab. 2:9).
10.   He is murderous and unmerciful (Hab. 2:12).
11.   He takes advantage of others (Hab. 2:15).
12.   He is violent and lustful.

Paul was making reference to this when he said, **"who hold the truth in unrighteousness."** We have many today that are holding the promises of God in unrighteousness! They have no concept or commitment to walking in true biblical holiness or righteousness. <u>All promises and no commandments will lead you directly into becoming the man in verse 5</u>! Is this the Laodicean Church in Revelation 3:14-22?

Revelation 3:14-22 (KJV)
[14] And unto the angel of the church of the Laodiceans write; These things saith the

---

[20] Strong's Enhanced Lexicon. BibleWorks for Windows 7.0. BibleWorks, LLC, Norfolk, VA. Copyright © 2006.
[21] Dake's Annotated Reference Bible: Containing the Old and New Testaments of the Authorized or King James Version Text.

Amen, the faithful and true witness, the beginning of the creation of God; [15] I know thy works, that thou art neither cold nor hot: I would thou wert cold or hot. [16] So then because thou art lukewarm, and neither cold nor hot, I will spue thee out of my mouth. [17] Because thou sayest, I am rich, and increased with goods, and have need of nothing; and knowest not that thou art wretched, and miserable, and poor, and blind, and naked: [18] I counsel thee to buy of me gold tried in the fire, that thou mayest be rich; and white raiment, that thou mayest be clothed, and *that* the shame of thy nakedness do not appear; and anoint thine eyes with eyesalve, that thou mayest see. [19] As many as I love, I rebuke and chasten: be zealous therefore, and repent. [20] Behold, I stand at the door, and knock: if any man hear my voice, and open the door, I will come in to him, and will sup with him, and he with me. [21] To him that overcometh will I grant to sit with me in my throne, even as I also overcame, and am set down with my Father in his throne. [22] He that hath an ear, let him hear what the Spirit saith unto the churches.

Maybe the pathway to lukewarmness is all promises and no commandments!

> **When we are faithful to the commandments of God, THEN God is faithful in keeping His promises to us!**

III.   A Clean Heart

1 John 3:18-24 (KJV)
[18] My little children, let us not love in word, neither in tongue; but in deed and in truth. [19] And hereby we know that we are of the truth, and shall assure our hearts before him. [20] For if our heart condemn us, God is greater than our heart, and knoweth all things. [21] Beloved, if our heart condemn us not, *then* have we confidence toward God. [22] ***And whatsoever we ask, we receive of him, because we keep his commandments, and do those things that are pleasing in his sight.*** [23] And this is his commandment, That we should believe on the name of his Son Jesus Christ, and love one another, as he gave us commandment. [24] And he that keepeth his commandments dwelleth in him, and he in him. And hereby we know that he abideth in us, by the Spirit which he hath given us.

1.   Our ability to have confidence in our prayer life (i.e. standing on the promises of God and knowing that He hears us) is directly connected to keeping the commandments (plural) of God.

2.   Our faithfulness (fidelity) to God commands opens the door for His promises to be fulfilled in our lives!

3.   The first commandment (believe on the Lord Jesus) is the gateway commandment that opens us up to the commandments and blessings of God.

4.   Walking in the commandments enables us to abide in Messiah!

Review Questions

1. In what truth is the power of God contained?

2. In your own words, describe what "living by faith" means Hebraically.

3. "All promises and no commandments" leads to where?

4. 1 John 3:18-24 deals with both the commandments and prayer. How does he link the two?

Covenant Faith – Lesson Fourteen

Developing Covenant Faith – Part 2

I. The Measure of Faith

Romans 12:3 *Amplified*
"For by the grace (unmerited favor of God) given to me I warn everyone among you not to estimate and think of himself more highly than he ought [not to have an exaggerated opinion of his own importance], but to rate his ability in sober judgment, each according to the degree of faith apportioned by God to him."

There are several very important things in this verse of Scripture about faith and calling. Since we are training those for ministry, we will deal with both.

a.   Each one of us has very specific things that God has called us to do. With each office of ministry, there is an anointing to carry it out. Individuals called to a larger ministry will still have to develop their *faith*, but the *anointing* in their ministry will cause more to happen. Some are called to pastor 100, and some 10,000. The anointing for that office will help bring it to pass. Some lose out and have things fall apart because they tried to do it all on the anointing and never developed their faith. For those in ministry, we MUST develop our faith and learn to flow WITH the anointing.

b.   The Scripture here also tells us that God has given to each one of us a "degree" or "measure" of faith. At the point of salvation, the Holy Spirit deposits faith into your spirit man. This allows you to believe the Word and to be "born-again." We need to realize that all in the Body of Christ have faith, and we also need to learn to develop it!

II. The Seeds of Faith

a.   **Faith, Fasting, & Prayer**

Matthew 17:20-21 (KJV)
[20] And Jesus said unto them, Because of your unbelief: for verily I say unto you, If ye have faith as a grain of mustard seed, ye shall say unto this mountain, Remove hence to yonder place; and it shall remove; and nothing shall be impossible unto you. [21] Howbeit this kind goeth not out but by prayer and fasting.

In this situation, the disciples failed to cast a demon out of a young boy. Jesus rebukes the demon and it leaves the boy. He then tells His disciples that faith is like a "mustard seed," and just that size faith would move mountains. (He also stresses that faith may need prayer and fasting to aid in deliverance.)

b.   I believe that Jesus, in His reference to a mustard seed, was speaking of a teaching He gives in **Matthew 13:31-32**.

Matthew 13:31-32 (KJV)
[31] Another parable put he forth unto them, saying, The kingdom of heaven is like to a grain of mustard seed, which a man took, and sowed in his field: [32] Which indeed is the least of all seeds: but when it is grown, it is the greatest among herbs, and becometh a tree, so that the birds of the air come and lodge in the branches thereof.

The Kingdom of Heaven is as a *mustard seed*.   Although it is small, plant it and it will grow. So faith may start small, but as we feed it, water it and use it, it will grow exceedingly!

III.   Developing Your Faith

Feeding Your Faith

Galatians 5:22-23 (KJV)
[22] But the fruit of the Spirit is love, joy, peace, longsuffering, gentleness, goodness, faith, [23] Meekness, temperance: against such there is no law.

1 Corinthians 12:7-11 (KJV)
[7] But the manifestation of the Spirit is given to every man to profit withal. [8] For to one is given by the Spirit the word of wisdom; to another the word of knowledge by the same Spirit; [9] To another faith by the same Spirit; to another the gifts of healing by the same Spirit; [10] To another the working of miracles; to another prophecy; to another discerning of spirits; to another *divers* kinds of tongues; to another the interpretation of tongues: [11] But all these worketh that one and the selfsame Spirit, dividing to every man severally as he will.

We need to recognize the importance of faith. Faith is both a fruit of the Spirit (**Gal. 5:22-23** - Developmental Faith: Faith that can grow and mature) and a gift of the Spirit (**I Corinthians 12:9** - A supernatural temporary equipping with God's faith). The fruit of faith is grown and developed out of our spirit. The gift of faith can only increase in its operation as the Spirit of God wills and as we learn to flow with Him.

Romans 10:17 (KJV)
[17] So then faith *cometh* by hearing, and hearing by the word of God.

Romans 10:17- tells us that faith comes (or in the life of a believer further developed) by hearing the Word of God. The Word of God can feed faith much like food feeds our physical bodies.

Proverbs 4:20-23 (KJV)
[20] My son, attend to my words; incline thine ear unto my sayings. [21] Let them not depart from thine eyes; keep them in the midst of thine heart. [22] For they *are* life unto those that find them, and health to all their flesh. [23] Keep thy heart with all diligence; for out of it *are* the issues of life.

Proverbs 4:20-23 - When we attend to God's Word, it provides food for our faith, gives health to our flesh and causes life to SPRING forth from our hearts.

Psalm 1:2-3 (KJV)
[2] But his delight *is* in the law of the LORD; and in his law doth he meditate day and night. [3] And he shall be like a tree planted by the rivers of water, that bringeth forth his fruit in his season; his leaf also shall not wither; and whatsoever he doeth shall prosper.

Psalm 1:2-3 - Our faith-life can become established and stable through meditation and fellowship with the written Word of God.

Remember, you feed what you mediate upon. If you think on problems, they grow. If you think on God's Word and His faithfulness, faith will grow. To quote the late Dr. Sumrall: "Feed your faith and starve your doubts to death."

Steps in Meditating: When we think (meditate) upon the Word, always ask God two questions "why" and "how." Faith rises when we understand God's ways. When we understand why God does the things He does, we can flow with Him and work with Him. When we understand "how" He does things, we learn to do the works of Jesus as He promised we would do. Always ask God His logic behind what He tells us to do and then how to do it. When we do things His way, we will see great results.

IV. Water Your Faith

Luke 17:5 (KJV)
[5] And the apostles said unto the Lord, Increase our faith.

Matthew 17:21 (KJV)
[21] Howbeit this kind goeth not out but by prayer and fasting.

It is proper, when we are faced with hard situations, to seek the face of God and ask Him to increase our faith. I believe that this is also demonstrated when Jesus said that "some cannot come out (demons) without prayer and fasting." From this, I believe, faith is watered by the presence of God and strengthened by fasting.

The more we learn of God, the stronger faith becomes. As we spend time in His presence and learn of Him, we realize His greatness, His power and His faithfulness to His Word. It causes our confidence to grow in Him because of a deepening personal relationship.

Fasting is important. Our fleshly nature can stifle faith and choke it. Fasting disciplines the flesh and allows us to be more "spiritually" aware than "physically" aware. It shows our seriousness in the things of the Kingdom of God, and helps bring the "Spirit, Soul and Body" balance back to God's design for us.

V. Exercise Your Faith

When we plant faith as a seed, I am convinced this term means to use it. Faith, like a muscle, becomes stronger when we exercise it. If we are required by God to live by faith, that means we are using it daily for all things. Stretch your faith; begin believing for specific things. Start small and allow it to grow.

VI. Conclusion

As we apply these principles, we will begin to see our faith develop and grow. Jesus said "To him who has shall more be given, to him who has not what he has shall be taken away." In modern language we need to "use it or lose it"!

Review Questions

1.   Some Christians have faith and others don't. [ ] True [ ] False

2.   What are the three steps to maturing your faith?

Covenant Faith – Lesson Fifteen

The Boldness of Faith

I. The King Made a Decree - Bow or Burn

Daniel 3:10-11 (KJV)
[10] Thou, O king, hast made a decree, that every man that shall hear the sound of the cornet, flute, harp, sackbut, psaltery, and dulcimer, and all kinds of musick, shall fall down and worship the golden image: [11] And whoso falleth not down and worshippeth, *that* he should be cast into the midst of a burning fiery furnace.

The King made a decree that when the music sounded, all the world was to bow down to his idol. In much the same way, the World wants Christians to bow down to what they want rather than the Word of God. They say: "Bow down and compromise for what we want or pay the price!!" In today's world, the Christian and the Church are constantly being told to "bow or burn."

II. No Compromise

Daniel 3:16-18 (KJV)
[16] Shadrach, Meshach, and Abednego, answered and said to the king, O Nebuchadnezzar, we *are* not careful to answer thee in this matter. [17] If it be *so*, our God whom we serve is able to deliver us from the burning fiery furnace, and he will deliver *us* out of thine hand, O king. [18] But if not, be it known unto thee, O king, that we will not serve thy gods, nor worship the golden image which thou hast set up.

Faith will not compromise. Faith refuses to bow. Faith will always commit to God's Word, regardless of the circumstances.

Faith says "If you bow, you will burn."

III. Tactics of Satan

Satan tries to put us into circumstances where we have to compromise the Word of God. If we compromise, we are right where he wants us!

What we compromise to keep, we will always lose!

We can put pressure on the Devil by refusing to compromise and standing upon God's Word at all times!

IV. Pressure, No Problem!

2 Corinthians 11:23-28 (KJV)

[23] Are they ministers of Christ? (I speak as a fool) I *am* more; in labours more abundant, in stripes above measure, in prisons more frequent, in deaths oft. [24] Of the Jews five times received I forty *stripes* save one. [25] Thrice was I beaten with rods, once was I stoned, thrice I suffered shipwreck, a night and a day I have been in the deep; [26] *In* journeyings often, *in* perils of waters, *in* perils of robbers, *in* perils by *mine own* countrymen, *in* perils by the heathen, *in* perils in the city, *in* perils in the wilderness, *in* perils in the sea, *in* perils among false brethren; [27] In weariness and painfulness, in watchings often, in hunger and thirst, in fastings often, in cold and nakedness. [28] Beside those things that are without, that which cometh upon me daily, the care of all the churches.

Paul, having gone through all these things, could have easily compromised and said: "Well, maybe God didn't want me to take the Gospel to all the Gentiles. I'll just make tents from now on! Nobody gets mad at a fellow for making tents!"

V. II Timothy 3:11-12

2 Timothy 3:11-12 (KJV)

[11] Persecutions, afflictions, which came unto me at Antioch, at Iconium, at Lystra; what persecutions I endured: ***but out of them all the Lord delivered me.*** [12] Yea, and all that will live godly in Christ Jesus shall suffer persecution.

Persecution?   ---- Yes!
Deliverance from God? ----- Yes!

IV. Faith Demands Boldness

Acts 4:29-31 (KJV)

[29] And now, Lord, behold their threatenings: and grant unto thy servants, that with all boldness they may speak thy word, [30] By stretching forth thine hand to heal; and that signs and wonders may be done by the name of thy holy child Jesus. [31] And when they had prayed, the place was shaken where they were assembled together; and they were all filled with the Holy Ghost, and they spake the word of God with boldness.

When we are threatened by Satan, we need to ask God to stretch forth His hand in power and give us boldness!

Proverbs 28:1 (KJV)

[1] The wicked flee when no man pursueth: but the righteous are bold as a lion.

VII. Might

Ephesians 6:10 (KJV)
[10] Finally, my brethren, be strong in the Lord, and in the power of his might.

Might: **Strongs # G2479 ἰσχύς ischus {is-khoos'}** [22]
Meaning: 1) ability, force, strength, might
Origin: from a derivative of is (force, cf eschon, a form of 2192); TDNT - 3:397,378; n f
Usage: AV - strength 4, power 2, might 2, ability 1, mightily + 1722 1, mighty 1; 11
Misc: For Synonyms see entry 5820

His Might = the Ability to Do Anything

We need to learn to be strong in the might of God. It is not in our strength, talents or abilities, but only in God's power and might!

VIII. Refuse to Bow

Daniel 3:19-30 (KJV)
[19] Then was Nebuchadnezzar full of fury, and the form of his visage was changed against Shadrach, Meshach, and Abednego: *therefore* he spake, and commanded that they should heat the furnace one seven times more than it was wont to be heated. [20] And he commanded the most mighty men that *were* in his army to bind Shadrach, Meshach, and Abednego, *and* to cast *them* into the burning fiery furnace. [21] Then these men were bound in their coats, their hosen, and their hats, and their *other* garments, and were cast into the midst of the burning fiery furnace. [22] Therefore because the king's commandment was urgent, and the furnace exceeding hot, the flame of the fire slew those men that took up Shadrach, Meshach, and Abednego. [23] And these three men, Shadrach, Meshach, and Abednego, fell down bound into the midst of the burning fiery furnace. [24] Then Nebuchadnezzar the king was astonied, and rose up in haste, *and* spake, and said unto his counsellors, Did not we cast three men bound into the midst of the fire? They answered and said unto the king, True, O king. [25] He answered and said, Lo, I see four men loose, walking in the midst of the fire, and they have no hurt; and the form of the fourth is like the Son of God. [26] Then Nebuchadnezzar came near to the mouth of the burning fiery furnace, *and* spake, and said, Shadrach, Meshach, and Abednego, ye servants of the most high God, come forth, and come *hither*. Then Shadrach, Meshach, and Abednego, came forth of the midst of the fire. [27] And the princes, governors, and captains, and the king's counsellors, being gathered together, saw these men, upon whose bodies the fire had no power, nor was an hair of their head singed, neither were their coats changed, nor the smell of fire had passed on them. [28] *Then* Nebuchadnezzar spake, and said, Blessed *be* the God of Shadrach, Meshach, and Abednego, who hath sent his angel, and delivered his servants that trusted in him, and have changed the king's word, and yielded their bodies, that they might not serve nor worship any god, except their own God. [29] Therefore I make a decree, That every people, nation, and language, which speak any thing amiss against the God of Shadrach, Meshach, and Abednego, shall be cut in pieces, and their houses shall be made a dunghill: because there is no other God

---

[22] Strong's Enhanced Lexicon. BibleWorks for Windows 7.0. BibleWorks, LLC, Norfolk, VA. Copyright © 2006.

that can deliver after this sort. [30] Then the king promoted Shadrach, Meshach, and Abednego, in the province of Babylon.

Refuse to bow; victory is at hand!

Review Questions

1.   What is the world constantly pressuring believers to do?

_____
_____
_____
_____
_____
_____
_____
_____
_____

2.   What we compromise to keep, _____.

3.   How are we to respond to Satanic threats?

_____
_____
_____
_____
_____
_____
_____
_____
_____

4.   When we refuse to bow, _____ is a hand.

Covenant Faith – Lesson Sixteen

Faith is a Life of Making the Impossible Possible

I.   Believe the Possibilities

Mark 10:27 (KJV)
[27] And Jesus looking upon them saith, With men *it is* impossible, but not with God: for with God all things are possible.

Mark 9:23 (KJV)
[23] Jesus said unto him, If thou canst believe, all things *are* possible to him that believeth.

a.   In working in the Kingdom, possibilities are NEVER gauged by our own abilities.

b.   God will use our talents, BUT He is not limited to those talents.

c.   **God will take the "least-likely" and use them to change the world**! Moses spent 40 years believing that he was somebody. He then spent 40 years learning that he was nobody. Finally, he lived 40 years with the realization that God can use the ordinary for extraordinary things!

d.   We need to get our eyes off of our inability and fix our gaze on His limitless abilities.

e.   Our faith, trust, and belief in the power of God and His ability to accomplish what He promised, releases that ability into our lives.

f.   Belief is the key to open God's ability in our lives and ministries!

II.   God's Power Released to Bring About What He Wants

Psalm 37:3-6 (KJV)
[3] Trust in the LORD, and do good; *so* shalt thou dwell in the land, and verily thou shalt be fed. [4] Delight thyself also in the LORD; and he shall give thee the desires of thine heart. [5] Commit thy way unto the LORD; trust also in him; and he shall bring *it* to pass. [6] And he shall bring forth thy righteousness as the light, and thy judgment as the noonday.

a.   *"Trust in the Lord, and do good; Dwell in the land, and feed on His faithfulness."* - This verse speaks of entering an intimate relationship with God. This relationship is based upon TRUST. As I trust Him, I begin doing good (walking in the level of understanding and insight in the Word). As I do, I am nourished and sustained by the FAITHFULNESS of God.

b.   *"Delight yourself in the Lord, and He shall give you the desires of your heart."* - <u>Delight can be defined as "to take great pleasure or joy[23]."</u> As I take great pleasure and joy in my relationship with God, something begins to happen. No human can enter into this type of relationship with God and leave unchanged. My heart will begin to line up with the heart of God. His desires will become my desires. In other words, God will give new desires in my heart to fulfill His desires for my life and ministry.

c.   *"Commit your way to the Lord, Trust also in Him, and He shall bring it to pass."* - As God places new desires in my heart, they are always beyond my talents and abilities. When God dreams through us, He dreams big. His desire is not according to our abilities, but according to His. Therefore the only way to make it a reality is to totally commit to God. Every step must be led by His Spirit. His anointing must saturate everything if it is going to be productive. My trust (or confidence) cannot be in the flesh (my own abilities and talents) but must reside in God's abilities and faithfulness. As I do this, God will bring it to pass.

IV.   Running the Race

Hebrews 12:1-2 (KJV)
[1] Wherefore seeing we also are compassed about with so great a cloud of witnesses, let us lay aside every weight, and the sin which doth so easily beset *us*, and let us run with patience the race that is set before us, [2] Looking unto Jesus the author and finisher of *our* faith; who for the joy that was set before him endured the cross, despising the shame, and is set down at the right hand of the throne of God.

a.   <u>When God makes the impossible possible in our lives, it appears that God makes us extremists</u>. We begin laying aside everything that is not important for what God wants. First, it's sins and snares: things Satan will use to hold us back. Then it is things that are not necessarily sin but are no longer necessary. Our desires and passions have changed. Those old things that once were important to us no longer hold the same meaning. God's power, presence and anointing hold a higher importance than anything else this world has to offer us.

b.   We need to keep our eyes on Jesus. This will get us through the hard times and keep us on course. We should not even keep our eyes on the desires that God is having us accomplish. Only keep our eyes on Jesus. Why? Those desires and projects can become gods to us. Otherwise our relationship with God is not pushing us on – it's our own relationship to the project, desire or dream.

Remember, man's soul is more important that any plan or project in the Kingdom of God. God will trash a project or ministry to save the man!

c.   Jesus is the author and finisher (or developer) of our faith. We need to invite Jesus to develop and bring our faith to maturity. Only He can do it. There may be parts He needs to

---

[23] *The American Heritage® Dictionary of the English Language, Third Edition* copyright © 1992 by Houghton Mifflin Company. Electronic version licensed from InfoSoft International, Inc. All rights reserved.

stretch, sand down, tack up and refinish. But only He can do it. Allow Him free reign in your life to get it done.

d.   "who for the joy that was set before Him, endured the cross, despising the shame…" Jesus was able to complete the work the Father had for Him because He kept His eyes on the Father and then the task. It allowed Him to go through a time of fame and not get "big headed." And it also allowed Him to go through a time of shame and despair and not lose hope. THE ONLY WAY WE CAN KEEP OUR STRENGTH IS TO KEEP OUR EYES ON JESUS AND STAY BALANCED.

Review Questions

1.   When we work in the Kingdom, whose abilities should we be looking at?

2.   Explain in your own words what Psalms 37:3-6 means.

3.   When God really starts moving in our lives, why do we look like extremists?

_____

4.   Why is keeping our eyes on Jesus so important?

_____

Bibliography

The American Heritage® Dictionary of the English Language, Third Edition copyright © 1992 by Houghton Mifflin Company. Electronic version licensed from InfoSoft International, Inc. All rights reserved.

Dake's Annotated Reference Bible: Containing the Old and New Testaments of the Authorized or King James Version Text.

Dewalt, Michael. The Self-Sufficiency of God. Article. http://gospelcenteredmusings.com/2009/11/11/the-self-sufficiency-of-god/

R. Laird Harris, Gleason L. Archer, Bruce K. Waltke, ed., *Theological Wordbook of the Old Testament*, (Chicago: Moody Press, 1980), WORD*search* CROSS e-book.

Kottke, Chad. Restoring Foundations: Rediscovering Truths of Covenant and Torah. Thesis submitted to Biblical Life College and Seminary toward the Master of Divinity degree. Copyright 2011.

The New Pilgrim Bible KJV Student Edition. Oxford University Press, Oxford, NY. © Copyright 1948, 1976, 2003.

Covenant Faith Answer Key

Lesson 1

1. God did not need creation for Himself. He created because of grace. That grace spoke commandments to the chaos that covered the earth and brought divine order.

2. Yes. Be fruitful. Replenish the earth. Subdue it. Take dominion over creation. Cultivate the Garden and protect it. Do not eat of the tree of the Knowledge of Good and Evil.

3. To be filled with the Spirit of God and to function within God's commandments.

Lesson 2

1. By throwing out biblical concepts we do not like and overemphasizing concepts beyond their original balance.

2. No. Covenant requires the shedding of blood to create. Adam had a divine commission before the fall. Covenant was only established after the fall.

3. Grace always comes first, then commandments. Paul was dealing in Eph. 2:8-10 with the erroneous concept of salvation through circumcision.

Lesson 3

1. Doing commandments.

2. Loving instruction (as a father to a son) and direction.

3. Yes. He heard God's instruction and built an ark. His obedience built a place of safety for his family.

Lesson 4

1. To help us grow into who we really are in Christ.

2. By embedding Babylon into the concepts of the church.

3. Wealth and material belonging can buy influence and make it appear that God is blessing something when He is not.

Lesson 5

1. It begins where man's abilities end.

2.   Yes. It is the biblical pattern. Satan is hoping we will become offended at God's Word or so tangled up in this world that it chokes out the promise!

3.   We need to make sure our hearts are good ground and that we have God's Word (and His promises) deep within our hearts.

Lesson 6

1.   Yes. Even Abram had to deal with those.

2.   God's grace treats us like we are already there. God will intervene and help to bring us to the place His grace is taking us.

3.   God cannot hear us at the place of disobedience. We must repent and return to where we left God to continue the journey with Him.

Lesson 7

1.   Overcoming strife.

2.   It is a place where you are walking in love for God, His Word, and His commandments.

3.   It allows the enemy to take us captive at his will, and it will de-energize our faith.

4.   It energizes our faith, drives out fear, and places us in a good position for victory.

5.   Love must take us beyond our need of the moment to be used by God in this world.

6.   God always expands our vision.

Lesson 8

1.   He used them to build his household and his defenses. He was prepared for the time of trouble.

2.   It came after his greatest victory.

3.   It was the mystery of the bread and wine (communion).

4.   In the Ev' Shabbat Meal and in the Passover Meal.

Lesson 9

1.   We can be tempted by the riches of the world rather than the blessing of God.

2.   I (God) was your shield during battle and I (God) am your reward!

3.

His Seed: Abram, the promise is going to be your seed. What I am doing in your heart is so great, it cannot help but produce!

His Vision: Look at all the stars in the heavens. Try your best to number them. That is how many descendants you will eventually have!

His Faith: Right here is where we establish the pattern of entering into what God and Abram would do. Abram believed God when it looked impossible.

4.   Satan must water down or get you off to keep the full impact of the covenant from being established.

Lesson 10

1.   They cause us to use worldly and Babylonian ways in an attempt to fulfill the promises of God.

2.   It will always raise up to mock the fulfillment by God.

3.   God told Abram: "Come walk with Me and I will make you complete, whole, and sound.

Lesson 11

1.   In this new covenant relationship, it was Abraham's responsibility to welcome God in and to make Him feel welcomed. (Just like us today.)

2.   Because of covenant, Abraham walked in righteousness. This allowed him to sit as a judge through intercession.

3.   Abraham stood between the LORD and Sodom and Gomorrah. God had to look to him first as he interceded before He could look at these cities.

Lesson 12

1.   Tempting is to entice someone to sin. Testing is to prove the ability and maturity of someone.

2.   It was on the third day Abraham saw the place. He also said that both he and the boy would go up and come back down.

3.   He opened the door that allowed God to offer His Son for mankind (and on the very same spot)!

Lesson 13

1.   The Gospel that includes the death, burial, and resurrection of Jesus.

2.	To be firm, steadfast and have fidelity in the ways of God.

3.	To becoming the Laodicean Church.

4.	Our prayers are heard because of our faithfulness to His commandments and doing those things that are pleasant in His sight.

Lesson 14

1.	False

2.	Meditating on the Word, watering the Word through prayer and fasting, and exercising our faith (using it daily.)

Lesson 15

1.	To compromise God's Word

2.	We will always lose.

3.	Be bold and refuse to compromise.

4.	Victory.

Lesson 16

1.	God's ability.

2.	Compare to topic # 2 in lesson.

3.	We begin laying aside everything that holds us back and have a singular focus on God and His purposes.

4.	As the author and finisher of our faith, He keeps us balanced. He also gives us strength to push through to victory.

Made in United States
North Haven, CT
25 November 2024

60921709R00046